ANGRY AFRICA

ANGRY AFRICA

A Study on Post-Colonialism and How "France-Afrique" Policy Led to Anti-French Coups

HICHEM KAROUI

Global East-West (London)

CONTENTS

CHAPTER 1

Preface

Under the government of President Emmanuel Macron, the French African policy, which is known as Francafrique and was initially implemented by President Charles de Gaulle, has, in fact, been confronted with significantly more difficult issues. The tenure of Macron has been marked by a series of protests and revolts in various African countries, expressing a rising unhappiness with France's influence and policies in the region. These events have occurred in a number of African countries.

French President Emmanuel Macron has made an effort to rethink France's connection with Africa by claiming that the period of Francafrique has come to an end and that France does not have a policy regarding Africa.In an effort to establish a new foundation for relations with African states, he has acknowledged the wrongs that were committed during the colonial era, returned cultural treasures, and even agreed to do away with the CFA franc, which is a currency that is related to France and is used by eight West African nations. Despite these attempts, his policies have been met with a variety of responses, and his initiatives have been criticised of lacking credibility with regard to their trustworthiness.

There have been a number of variables that have contributed to the current impasse. In addition to being accused of being racist by a number of African pundits, Macron's direct manner and the impression that he is condescending have been taken into criticism. The continued military actions in the Sahel region, which have been generally failed and unpopular, have damaged his efforts to improve the relationship. His efforts have caused the relationship to become more strained. In addition, military juntas in Mali, Burkina Faso, and Niger have taken advantage of anti-French sentiment in order to resist the policies that Macron has implemented.

Additionally, the growing influence of other global powers in Africa, such as China and Russia, has made Macron's plans more difficult to implement. French President Emmanuel Macron has accused these countries of rekindling long-standing disagreements on sovereignty and colonial exploitation, which has further strained France's relations with African nations.

In conclusion, despite the fact that Macron has implemented measures with the intention of redefining and modernising France's relationship with Africa, these policies have been received with tremendous resistance and criticism. This has led to what is believed to be an impasse, with protests and revolts taking place in a number of African countries, suggesting a rising unhappiness with France's power and policies in the region.

Emmanuel Macron has issued a number of remarks and taken actions to address the concerns that have been raised in reaction to the ongoing demonstrations against his Africa policy. He has declared on multiple occasions that the period of French meddling in Africa has come to an end, which indicates a move away from France's post-colonial relationship with the continent he is referring to. Macron has also made efforts to revitalise France's connection with Africa, highlighting the fact that the continent is a political priority for his presidency. Macron has refuted allegations that he is racist and condescending, despite the fact that he has made statements that contradict these allegations. There have been demonstrations against Macron's travels in a number of African nations, including the Congo, where some inhabitants have expressed the opinion that they have been victimised by France's policies. Macron has acknowledged France's colonial past and its mistreatment of Algerians in an effort to reset France's relationship with Africa. This is part of Macron's effort to reset it. He has also established a panel to investigate the massacres that occurred during the colonial era in Cameroon4. In Africa, Macron has made an effort to connect with young people, members of civil society, and new companies, sometimes going around African governments. As part of his agreement to return cultural riches to Africa, he has also decided to do away with the CFA franc, which is a currency that is related to France and is used by eight countries in West Africa. In spite of this, the effoJanu29artrts taken have not been sufficient to put an end to the complaints and demonstrations. Anti-French sentiment has been observed in a number of African nations, which has been fostered by the belief that France is interfering in political affairs and that France maintains a military presence in the Sahel region. Macron has outlined his vision of a revitalised cooperation with Africa, in which the continent is on equal footing with France, as a reaction to the difficulties that have been presented. He has made an effort to remove the notion that France is a proud nation that was once a colonial power, and he has emphasised his dedication to being a business partner for the long term. A number of groups that are contributing to instability in the region, including as the M23 rebel group in Congo, have been criticised by Macron.

The following are some of the reforms that Macron has actually made or proposed:

There will be a decrease in France's military presence in Africa, with a "noticeable reduction" in personnel numbers, and there will be a change towards a partnership-based approach to security.

The transition to a paradigm in which facilities are "co-administered" with local troops, which will result in the end of France's practice of hosting conventional military posts in Africa.

An admission of France's colonial past and its maltreatment of Algerians, as well as the establishment of a commission to investigate colonial massacres in Cameroon, are both things that should be done.

An initiative that has already resulted in the return of some things to African countries, with the goal of returning cultural treasures to those countries.

There is an emphasis placed on connecting with young people, civic society, and startup companies in Africa, often going around the established routes of government.

The elimination of the CFA franc, a currency that was linked to France and was utilised by eight countries in West Africa, symbolises a step towards greater economic autonomy for these countries.

The policies of Macron continue to be met with hostility and scepticism, notwithstanding the adjustments that have been made. Those who are opposed to the adjustments claim that they are either insufficient or should be interpreted as strategic communication rather than actual transformation.

Protests against Macron's Africa policy indicate that there is a significant level of dissatisfaction with France's influence and policies in the region. It is yet to be determined whether Macron's adjustments will be sufficient to address these concerns and reshape France's relationship with Africa in a manner that is regarded as more equitable and respectful by African nations and the citizens of those nations within those nations.

H.Karoui

Quillan, 29 January 2024.

CHAPTER 2

The Causes of Frequent Military Coups in Africa

A Sociopolitical Analysis

Military coups in Africa, a recurring issue in the continent's postcolonial history, have piqued the interest of academics, policymakers, and observers worldwide. The phenomenon's prevalence has been attributed to numerous variables. According to some researchers, the history of colonialism and the arbitrary borders imposed by European powers resulted in ethnically diverse states, making governance difficult. Furthermore, economic constraints, a lack of democratic traditions, and Cold War politics all played essential roles in the power dynamics of many African countries. Adopting an interdisciplinary approach incorporating political science, history, and sociology is critical for understanding African military coups. This enables a more nuanced examination of the various reasons for each coup, going beyond simple numbers.

MILITARY COUPS IN AFRICA: A HISTORICAL OVERVIEW

With its rich tapestry of sociopolitical histories and postcolonial experiences, the African continent has witnessed several military coups since the mid-20th century. Understanding the origin and the subsequent frequency of these coups provides a vantage point from which we can analyse the continent's evolving political landscape.

Origin of Military Coups in Africa

There were no military coups in Africa before 1952. It was in Egypt that everything began. On July 23, 1952, the first army coup in postcolonial Africa occurred. The Egyptian Free Officers Movement, under the leadership of General Muhammad Naguib and later Lieutenant Colonel Gamal Abdel Nasser, successfully overthrew King Farouk's monarchy, ending the monarchy that had existed since 1805. [1] This coup was the first in Africa's long line of military coups.[2] This ushered in a new era in African politics, in which military interventions became commonplace.

Quantifying Military Coups in Africa Since 1952

Until 2021, there were over 200 coup attempts in Africa, with more than half succeeding. However, distinguishing between attempted and successful coups is critical. The former refers to military actions that tried to usurp power but did not always result in a change of government. In contrast, the latter resulted in the removal of the current ruler. These military operations have not been dispersed equitably across the continent. Several coups have occurred in countries such as Benin, Nigeria, and Burkina Faso, while others have had a more stable political history.

According to some estimates, military coups have been common in Africa since the 1950s, with a success rate of more than 40% since 1958. West Africa serves as the primary hub of coup activity.

The major findings of a recent study,[3] are that military interventions have continued to be pervasive in Africa, despite democratisation trends since 1990; that coups, failed coups, and coup plots form a syndrome of military-led Elite political instability (PI); that colonial heritage is unrelated to coup activity; that the chance of success when launching a coup attempt has averaged more than 40% since 1958; that once a successful coup has occurred, military factionalism often leads to more coup behaviour; that except for a declining rate of success once a coup is undertaken, there is no major difference between 1956–79 and 1980–2001; that no trends of increasing or decreasing coup behaviour are evident, except that up to around 1975, as decolonisation progressed,

Total Military Intervention Score (TMIS) also increased; and that West Africa is the predominant centre of coup activity in sub-Saharan African (SSA), although all African regions have experienced coups.[4]

Of 486 attempted or successful coups worldwide since 1950, Africa has seen 214, the most of any region, with 106 successful. This data is based on research compiled by American researchers Jonathan M. Powell and Clayton L. Thyne. [5] At least 45 of the 54 nations across the African continent have experienced at least a single coup attempt since 1950.[6]

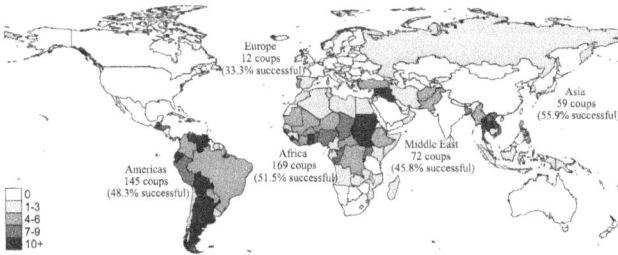

Figure 1. Instances of coup attempts, 1950 to 2010

Figure 1. Source: Powell and Thyne (2011)

Region	Coup attempts	Successful	Failed
Africa	214	106	108
Latin America	146	70	76
East Asia	49	27	22
Middle East	44	21	23
Europe	17	8	9
South Asia	16	10	6
Global	486	242	244

WHY SO MANY COUPS IN AFRICA?

Military coups in Africa occur as a result of several circumstances. Weak democratic infrastructure, residues of authoritarianism, and democratic failure contribute to coup recurrence.[7] Furthermore, disenchantment with democracy's promise of wealth and higher living standards, combined with social, economic, security, and political issues, has resulted in cordial acceptance and support for military takeovers in some African countries.[8] Diversifying military and civilian governments and weak political and institutional organisations create favourable conditions for coups.[9] The return of coups in West Africa has been particularly concerning, with repercussions for the region's peace, security, and stability.[10] To prevent coups, it is necessary to institutionalise governance and address sociopolitical, economic, and human security considerations that justify the military assault on power.[11] Strengthening sub-regional democracy, supporting good governance, and addressing leadership difficulties are critical in preventing coups.

According to Collier and Hoeffler (2005), the causes of coups and civil conflicts in Africa are similar, with low income and a lack of economic growth as common contributors. Standard indicators of discontent, such as political repression and economic inequality, have little influence on the probability of coups. Further events are more likely to occur after a coup or civil war, indicating the existence of "traps" in the system. Policies favouring the military do not reduce the likelihood of military coups; in fact, excessive military spending may increase the likelihood of coups.[12]

Six Major Factors

Based on the previous analysis, we retain six significant factors explaining the recurrence of the coups. They are as follows:

1. **Historical Context: Colonialism's Legacies**
   Africa's political structures and dynamics bear the indelible trace of its colonial past. Colonial powers' arbitrary demarcation of boundaries during the Scramble for Africa in the late 19th century led to the amalgamation of diverse ethnic, religious, and linguistic groups under singular administrative units.[13] Given the inherent ethnic and regional tensions, many nations

struggled with nation-building upon attaining independence.

2. **Weaknesses of Post-colonial States' Structure**
Many African states confronted the Herculean task of crafting a national identity, constructing solid institutions, and fostering a culture of democratic governance following independence. In numerous instances, institutions and the rule of law were fragile.[14] This institutional fragility frequently spawned vacuums that military entities attempted to fill with their organised structures.

3. **Economic Difficulties and Resource Distribution**
Repeatedly, economic hardships, frequently exacerbated by global economic downturns, unequal resource distribution, and pervasive corruption, have sparked social unrest.[15] When financial resources are scarce or controlled by a small elite, the military – often one of the better-funded institutions – may perceive itself as a corrective force, restoring order and redistributing resources.

4. **Influence from the Outside**
During the Cold War, superpowers supported specific regimes or opposition groups based on their ideological alignments. Frequently, these geopolitical diversions destabilise governments, making them susceptible to coups.[16] In the contemporary context, global powers continue

to exert influence, inadvertently nurturing conditions favourable to coups on occasion.

5. **The military as the "Guardians" of the state**
   In many African nations, the military is viewed not only as a defence force but also as the nation's "guardians." In conjunction with historical precedents, this self-assigned role has frequently legitimised the military's political involvement. [17]

6. **Expectations and Acceptance in Society**
   Due to historical or cultural factors, society may regard the military as a stabilising force in specific contexts. This societal acquiescence or expectation can provide the legitimacy necessary for the military to intervene in political processes.[18]

Therefore, military coups in Africa result from a complex interaction between historical legacies, institutional vulnerabilities, economic challenges, and societal dynamics. While efforts are being made to foster stable democratic institutions across the continent, it is essential to comprehend the underlying causes of these coups to develop effective solutions. Recognising the diversity of the African continent, it is necessary to remember that each country has its dynamics and that sweeping generalisations may only sometimes capture the nuances at play.

Finally, while the Egyptian coup in 1952 marked the beginning of a tumultuous political era in Africa, the reasons behind each subsequent coup are multifaceted and rooted in local and global sociopolitical contexts. Continuous research and updates are necessary to keep abreast of the changing political landscape of this diverse continent.

CHAPTER 3

An Examination of the Anti-French Trend

Dealing with military coups is not the same as dealing with civilian uprisings and revolts. A coup's social structure is oligarchic, implying a dictatorship in the making instead of a civilian outcry. Given the setting of these coups in four African countries, can we speak of an anti-democratic or anti-French trend motivating them?

We should first attempt to comprehend the underlying reasons and patterns. As discussed in the previous section, coups in Africa have been fueled by various variables such as power disputes, ethnic tensions, economic inequities, and outsider meddling. Anti-democratic and anti-French attitudes are prevalent in the countries above.

1. Anti-Democratic Trends:

Over the previous few decades, the African continent has undergone both democratic growth and regression:

- Democratic Stagnation: Initial democratic progress in several countries in the 1990s and early 2000s has stalled or reversed. The continuance of authoritarian authority, often disguised as electoral democracy, can be discouraging for pro-democratic forces [19].
- The Role of the Military: In many states, the military remains a potent political actor. It frequently rationalises its actions as required to maintain order or battle corruption, even if they impair democratic procedures [20].

In the specific cases of these countries:

- Mali has experienced repeated coups in recent history, reflecting both internal security issues (such as Islamist insurgencies) and political unrest.
- Burkina Faso has also had previous coups and popular uprisings, with the military intervening when there is a political vacuum or turmoil.
- Niger and Gabon have histories of authoritarian leadership, with brief periods of democratic administration that have not always been permanent or fully institutionalised.

2. Anti-French Sentiments:

- Colonial Heritage: French colonialism has left a mixed legacy in these countries. While there are significant cultural, economic, and occasionally political ties to

France, there is also hatred of perceived neocolonialism [21].

- Military Presence: France's military actions in combating Islamist groups, particularly in Mali and Niger under Operation Barkhane, have been a subject of dispute. While some people appreciate the security help, others see it infringing on their sovereignty.
- Economic Relations: Economic linkages, such as the CFA franc's relationship with the French treasury, have been criticised as emblems of French supremacy in several West and Central African countries.

Given this background, anti-French sentiments may not be the primary motivator behind these coups, but they can serve as a catalyst or rhetorical weapon for mobilisation. It is critical to take a measured attitude to the events in Mali, Burkina Faso, Niger, and Gabon. While anti-democratic and anti-French attitudes exist in these circumstances, each country's political dynamics are distinct. The coups symbolise more significant problems to democratic consolidation and state sovereignty in the region, with external influences such as French intervention adding another degree of complication. The fact that France's policy in Africa (France-Afrique) is now considered the problem, not its solution, as we will show, should not be overlooked for, in our analysis, it is responsible for France's humiliation.

Since most of its African colonies attained independence in 1960, France has intervened militarily more than 50 times.[22] French military interventions in Africa frequently adhere to a coherent logic that prioritises the protection of local and regional political regimes, often at the expense of decent governance and long-term stability.[23] Many observers know that French protection, or even the appearance of it, has allowed many of these regimes to continue corrupt, discriminatory, and occasionally genocidal policies.[24]

Macron Does Not Trust Huntington

Political observers of Africa's democratic transitions and consolidation are now debating the future of African democracy thirty years after the publication of Huntington's *Democracy's Third Wave*.[25]

Examining more than 30 countries in Southern Europe, Latin America, East Asia, and Eastern Europe that transitioned from autocratic to democratic governments between 1974 and 1990, Huntington claims the current transitions are the third significant wave of democratisation in the modern world. *Each of the preceding two waves was followed by a reversal wave in which some countries returned to authoritarian rule.*

Huntington explains why and how the third wave occurred using actual instances, facts, and close analysis. The legitimacy dilemmas of authoritarian regimes; economic and social development; the changed role of the Catholic Church; the impact of the United States, the European Community, and the Soviet Union; and the "snowballing" phenomenon: change in one country stimulating change in others are all factors responsible for the democratic trend. Huntington contends that disillusionment with democracy is vital for democratic consolidation.

It is an opinion that, like other opinions of the same author, did not go without controversies.

But if Huntington is right about the "third wave," France should be the first to support the coups in its former African colonies as a "consolidation of democracy". Instead, we see Paris threatening with extreme measures and pushing (ECOWAS) for external military intervention. Obviously, Mr Macron does not trust Huntington!

Questioning France's Policies

Recent coups in Burkina Faso, Niger, Mali, and Gabon have cast doubt on the efficiency of "France-Afrique" policy, as all of them are tied up to France. For many observers, the coups in these former French colonies demonstrate France's diminishing influence in the region [26] and its policy's contribution to the loss of hope in the capacity of democracy to build a future for those African nations. This becomes clear if we examine the positions of the military leaders who took over and their supporters on the streets.

The junta leader in Burkina Faso has opposed French policies rather than the French people, criticising the country's previous relationship with France and the agreements that impeded its development.[27] In this country, the coup is believed to be driven by a deepening security crisis and the inability to control Islamist groups.[28]

Similarly, Operation Barkhane, France's military intervention in Mali, has been deemed a failure, as it degenerated into a protracted conflict with no apparent resolution.[29] Weak democratic institutions and tension between the military and civilian government contributed to the coup in this country[30].

In Niger, the coup resulted from a continually deteriorating security situation and the presence of foreign forces[31]. The coup has caused tensions between France and the United States, as France refused to engage diplomatically with the junta and backed a regional organisation (ECOWAS) that has threatened military intervention. [32]

The coup in Gabon has been compared to Zimbabwe's coup in 2017, which ousted President Robert Mugabe in favour of an ally, Emmerson Mnangagwa.[33] Dissatisfaction with the government (accused of corruption and mismanagement), President Ali Bongo's deteriorating health, and the influence of neighbouring countries have been evoked as factors driving the last coup in this country.

Recently, France has been described as a country "experiencing a historical anachronism" because it is attributed to powers that no longer exist.[34] Macron has called for a new, balanced relationship with Africa, emphasising a partnership-based approach and the co-administration of military bases with local personnel.[35] However, recent coups in these African nations cast doubt on the efficacy of Macron's African policy. Moreover, African presidents can now choose which global powers are more accommodating, including China, the United States, Russia, etc.

WHY ARE THEY IMPORTANT TO FRANCE?

Country	Muslim Demog. (% of the population)	GDP (2021 estimate)	Trade Balance with France (2021 est.)	National Currency	Principal Mineral Resources
Mali	95%	USD 17.51 Billion	– USD 0.15 Billion (2021 est.)	West African CFA franc (XOF)	Gold, phosphates, kaolin, salt, limestone, uranium, gypsum, granite, hydropower, bauxite, iron ore, manganese, tin and copper deposits
Burkina Faso	61.6%	USD 15.75 Billion	–USD 0.10 Billion	West African CFA franc (XOF)	Gold, Zinc, Manganese, limestone, marble; phosphates, pumice, salt
Niger	99%	USD 9.87 Billion	–USD 0.11 Billion	West African CFA franc (XOF)	Uranium ore; coal; iron ore; tin; phosphates; gold; molybdenum; gypsum, limestone
Gabon	12% (Muslims, mostly Christians)	USD 14.56 Billion	+USD 0.50 Billion	Central African CFA franc (XAF)	Crude oil, gold, timber, manganese and uranium deposits

Sources: a compilation from the World Bank, the World Factbook, BBC World-Africa.

Analytical Remarks

Muslim Demographics: With a clear majority in Burkina Faso, Muslim populations predominate in Mali and Niger, influencing the cultural, social, and occasionally political landscape. Gabon's population, on the other hand, is predominantly Christian, with a small Muslim minority.

GDP: Despite having a smaller population than Mali and Burkina Faso, Gabon has a higher GDP, mainly owing to its vast oil reserves. Significant resource richness, such as gold in Mali and Burkina Faso, contributes significantly to their GDPs.

Trade Balance with France: Except for Gabon, all countries have a trade deficit with France. Its oil exports most likely impact Gabon's trade surplus. This economic relationship may influence the political dynamics between these countries and their previous colonial power.

National Currency: Using the CFA franc in these countries indicates economic integration and alignment with the larger West and Central African economic regions and France, which guarantees the currency.

Principal Mineral Resources: These countries' enormous mineral resources, particularly gold and uranium, make them critical interests in the global arena. Such riches can be both a blessing and a curse, drawing international investment while posing the risk of resource-driven disputes and power struggles.

In a broader analytical context, the economic parameters of these nations should be instrumental in understanding their political stability. But that is not the case. Mineral wealth can occasionally lead to unequal distribution, which fosters unrest. Furthermore, the region's historical and present relations with France, as indicated by trade balances and currency affiliations, play an essential role in the region's geopolitical tapestry. That's why we need to delve a little more into that relationship.

France-Mali Bilateral Trade (Graphic 1)
Key Takeaways

France is a major exporter to Mali, and its main products are packaged medicaments, wheat, and combustion engines.

Mali's exports to France have decreased over the years, with the main products being oily seeds, insect resins, and other processed fruits and nuts.

Regarding economic complexity and total exports, France outperforms Mali significantly, with France ranking higher in both categories.

Graphic (1) Source: Observatory For Economic Complexity (OEC)

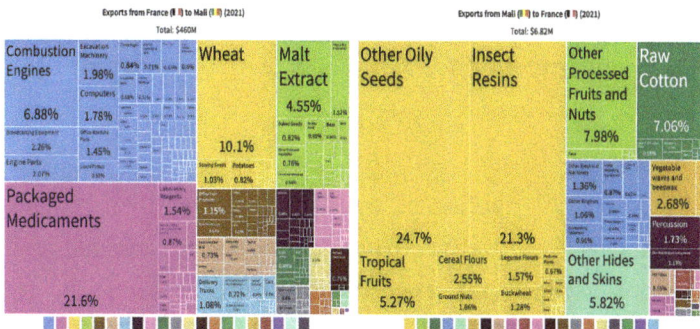

France exported $460M worth of goods to Mali in 2021, including packaged medicaments, wheat, and combustion engines. Over the past 26 years, France's exports to Mali have increased at an annualised rate of 3.87%. However, France did not export any services to Mali in 2021. On the other hand, Mali exported $6.82M worth of goods to France in 2021, such as other oily seeds, insect resins, and other processed fruits and nuts. Mali's exports to France have slightly decreased over the past 26 years.

Similarly, Mali did not export any services to France in 2021. Regarding economic complexity, France is ranked 15th with a higher Economic Complexity Index (ECI) and total exports of $569B, while Mali is ranked 125th with a lower ECI and total exports of $9.38B. Germany, Italy, and Belgium were the top countries importing more from France than Mali in 2021, while the United Arab Emirates imported more from Mali than France. Overall, France has a comparative advantage over Mali in certain products, as indicated in Graphic (1). **The economic competitiveness between the two countries is unbalanced.**

France-Burkina Faso Bilateral Trade (Graphic 2)
Key Takeaways

France has experienced consistent growth in its exports to Burkina Faso over the past 26 years, with packaged medicaments, wheat, and excavation machinery being the top products exported.

On the other hand, Burkina Faso's exports to France have

declined over the same period, with other pure vegetable oils, soybeans, and raw cotton being the major products exported.

France has a significantly higher economic complexity and total exports than Burkina Faso, indicating a stronger position in the global market.

Graphic (2) Source: Observatory For Economic Complexity (OEC)

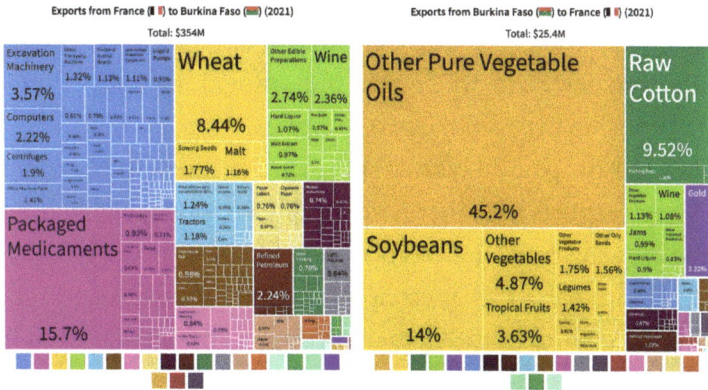

In 2021, France exported goods worth $354 million to Burkina Faso, including packaged medicaments, wheat, and excavation machinery. However, there were no service exports between the two countries. On the other hand, Burkina Faso exported goods worth $25.4 million to France, including vegetable oils, soybeans, and raw cotton. Over the past 26 years, France's exports to Burkina Faso have been increasing at an annualised rate of 3.58%, while Burkina Faso's exports to France have decreased at an annualised rate of 2.1%. France is ranked 15th in the Economic Complexity Index and has higher total exports than Burkina Faso, ranked 127th. **The economic competitiveness between the two countries is unbalanced.** (See Graphic 2).

France-Niger Bilateral Trade (Graphic 3)
Key Takeaways

France exported weapons parts and accessories, packaged medicaments, and other edible preparations to Niger, while Niger exported radioactive chemicals, uranium and thorium ore, and jewellery to France, indicating a significant trade relationship between the two countries.

Over the past 26 years, both France's exports to Niger and Niger's exports to France have steadily increased, highlighting the growing economic ties between the two nations.

France has a higher economic complexity index and total exports compared to Niger, indicating a stronger position in the global market, while Niger has shown a comparative advantage in exporting chemical products, precious metals, and metals to France.

Graphic (3) Source: Observatory For Economic Complexity (OEC)

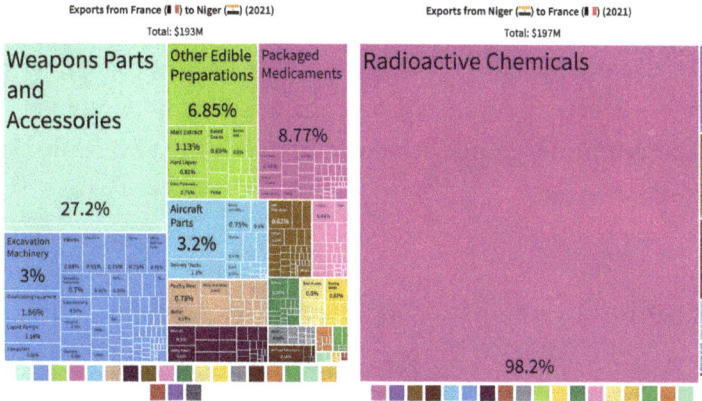

Exports from France (🇫🇷) to Niger (🇳🇪) (2021)
Total: $193M

Exports from Niger (🇳🇪) to France (🇫🇷) (2021)
Total: $197M

Weapons Parts and Accessories — 27.2%
Other Edible Preparations — 6.85%
Packaged Medicaments — 8.77%
Aircraft Parts — 3.2%
Excavation Machinery — 3%

Radioactive Chemicals — 98.2%

In 2021, France exported $193 million worth of goods to Niger, including weapons parts, packaged medicaments, and other edible preparations. Over the past 26 years, France's exports to Niger have increased at an annualised rate of 2.36%. However, France did not export any services to Niger in 2021. On the other hand, Niger exported $197 million worth of goods to France in 2021, mainly radioactive chemicals, uranium and thorium ore, and jewellery. Niger's exports to France have increased at an annualised rate of 1.38% over the past 26 years. Similarly, Niger did not export any services to France in 2021. When comparing the two countries' economic complexity and total exports, France ranked higher in both categories than Niger. France ranked 15th in the Economic Complexity Index. It had a total export value of $569 billion, while Niger ranked 90th in the Economic Complexity Index and had a total export value of $3.78 billion in 2021. Regarding trade between France and Niger, France had a net trade advantage in the export of weapons, machines, and foodstuffs, while Niger had a net trade advantage in the export of chemical products, precious metals, and metals. Overall, this data indicates that France has a comparative advantage over Niger in several product categories, as shown in Graphic (3). **The economic competitiveness between the two countries is unbalanced.**

France-Gabon Bilateral Trade (Graphic 4)
Key Takeaways

France has consistently increased its exports to Gabon over the past 26 years, with Packaged Medicaments, Wheat, and Malt Extract being the top exported products in 2021.

Gabon's exports to France have declined over the same period, with Veneer Sheets, Manganese Ore, and Crude Petroleum being the major products exported in 2021.

France is ranked higher in terms of economic complexity and total exports compared to Gabon, with Germany, Italy, and Belgium being the top importers of French goods.

Graphic (4) Source: Observatory For Economic Complexity (OEC)

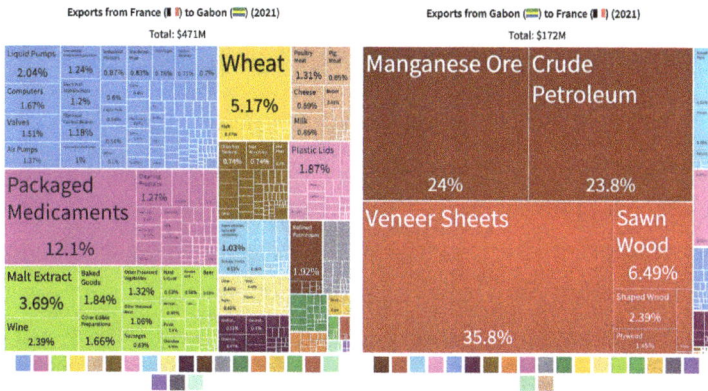

Exports from France (🇫🇷) to Gabon (🇬🇦) (2021)
Total: $471M

Exports from Gabon (🇬🇦) to France (🇫🇷) (2021)
Total: $172M

In 2021, France exported $471 million worth of goods to Gabon, including packaged medicaments, wheat, and malt extract. This represents an increase in exports over the past 26 years. However, France did not export any services to Gabon. On the other hand, Gabon exported $172 million worth of products to France, including veneer sheets, manganese ore, and crude petroleum. Gabon's exports to France have decreased over the past 26 years.

Regarding economic complexity and total exports, France ranked higher than Gabon in 2021. France had more imports from countries like Germany, Italy, and Belgium, while Gabon's leading importers were Sao Tome and Principe. Graphic (4) indicates that France has a comparative advantage over Gabon in certain products, while Gabon has its advantages in other areas. But still, **the economic competitiveness between the two countries is unbalanced.**

Results

None of these four African countries is satisfied with its bilateral trade with France, as none of them could even get closer to France's rank in the Economic Complexity Index. On the other hand, France has been more advantaged since the beginning, and its trade with them continually improved and expanded. The four countries have been an essential market for French products and a significant import source for various industries. The position of Niger is particularly noticeable, with more than 98 % of radio-active exports to France, including uranium and thorium.

CHAPTER 4

"France-Afrique" Policy

The term "Françafrique" was first used in 1955 by Félix Houphouët-Boigny, the first president of Ivory Coast. It refers to the close relationship between France and its former colonies in sub-Saharan Africa. The term was later shortened to "France-Afrique"[36].

Françafrique is often associated with neocolonialism, a former colonial power maintaining economic, political, or cultural influence over its former colony. France has been accused of using Françafrique to keep its African influence through economic aid, military intervention, and political interference. François Xavier Verschave, a French scholar, has intensively used the term Françafrique, spending much of his life exposing France's neocolonial projects in Africa. Verschave argued that Françafrique was a system of exploitation that benefited France at the expense of African countries.[37] Jacques Foccart, a French politician and advisor to French presidents Charles de Gaulle, Georges Pompidou (from 1960 to 1974), and Jacques Chirac, was instrumental in maintaining France's sphere of influence in Sub-Saharan Africa through a series of cooperation agreements covering political, economic, military, and cultural sectors with African countries.[38] In 1959, Foccart and Charles Pasqua co-founded the Gaullist Service d'Action Civique (SAC), which specialised in African covert operations. After de Gaulle, Foccart was considered the most powerful man in the Fifth Republic [39]. The term Françafrique is still used today to describe the relationship between France and its former African colonies. It is a complex and controversial issue, with many perspectives on its meaning and impact[40].

Under the France-Afrique policy, France considered itself a guarantor of regional stability and pursued an interventionist policy in Africa, culminating in an average of one military intervention per year from 1960 to the mid-1990s.[41]

France developed a massive empire in Africa during the colonial era, which had a tremendous impact on African nations and societies and French military, political, and economic institutions. Decolonisation in Africa was a complex process that differed by nation, with some countries attaining independence peacefully and others through protracted revolutions. France cultivated strong links with Sub-Saharan African governments when African countries declared independence.[42]

France maintained close relations with its former colonies after independence through political alliances, military and intelligence collaboration, and public development aid.[43] France also signed monetary cooperation treaties with three

African monetary regions: the West African Monetary and Economic Union (WAEMU), the Central African Economic and Monetary Community (CEMAC), and the Union of the Comoros.[44] These accords aided France's African partners' financial stability and supported strong, sustainable, and inclusive growth.[45] (See the graphic below).

France is linked to 15 African countries by monetary cooperation agreements

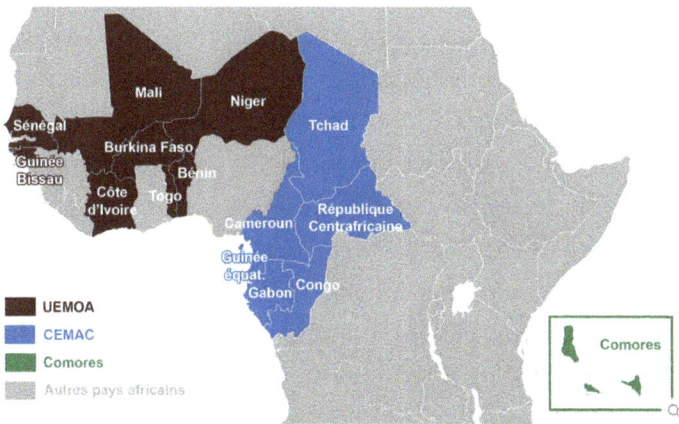

Figure 1. Source: Banque de France

Figure 1Source: Banque de France

The CFA franc is the currency of 14 African countries separated into two monetary unions. Benin, Burkina Faso, Côte d'Ivoire, Guinea-Bissau, Mali, Niger, Senegal, and Togo utilise the West African CFA franc (XOF). Cameroon, Central African Republic, Chad, Republic of the Congo, Equatorial

Guinea, and Gabon all use the Central African CFA franc (XAF)[46]. Although they are independent currencies, they have always been at parity and are essentially interchangeable[47]. They are tied to the euro and insured by the French treasury.

Nevertheless, the France-Afrique policy has been criticised for sustaining a paternalistic influence and quiet deal-making among elites and for military operations in former colonies.[48] Despite President Macron's efforts to re-establish France's ties with Africa, the policy continues encountering substantial challenges and criticism.[49]

For example, a CADTM article addresses the ongoing impact of France's imperialist monetary practises on its former African colonies.[50] It emphasises the CFA franc's significance in sustaining French sovereignty over these countries. According to the writers, France has always utilised threats, violence, and coercion to keep African governments aligned with French objectives. The colonial-era "cooperation agreements" of France allowed for minimal autonomy while maintaining control in Paris. Recent reforms to the CFA franc system, such as the transfer to the "eco" and the elimination of deposit obligations, are viewed as attempts to preserve indirect control. The French military presence in African countries continues to impact their decisions and actions. The essay refutes the claim that French aid compensates for its benefits through exploitative arrangements, arguing that compulsory deposits in the French treasury surpass aid contributions. The authors recommend that African countries desiring economic sovereignty should establish strategies relying on native resources rather than foreign cash, debt, and development aid. The relationship between French economic domination and African government corruption is discussed, with the system enabling corruption and subjugation.[51]

Is "France-Afrique" more of a neo-imperialist control structure than a win-win policy? That is the unavoidable question.

WHEN FRANCE-AFRIQUE IS PERCEIVED AS A SYSTEM OF CONTROL

France maintained control over its former African colonies via economic, political, and military methods. The CFA franc, a currency used in 14 former French colonies in West and Central Africa, is an integral part of this control. The CFA franc is pegged to the euro and guaranteed by the French government. Therefore, African countries must keep some foreign exchange reserves in France[52]. This system has been criticised for constraining these countries' economic autonomy and sustaining a sort of neocolonialism[53].

In addition to monetary control, France retains a considerable military presence in Africa, the most of any former colonial power. According to the Council on Foreign Relations, France has nearly 12,000 troops engaged in peacekeeping operations around the world, with nearly half of them deployed in Africa in both military and advisory capacities.[54] The French military has three main bases in Africa, with the largest being at Djibouti, and smaller forces at Dakar in Senegal and Libreville in Gabon. However, French President Emmanuel Macron has pledged to reduce France's military presence in

Africa.[55] As of 2023, France has about 3,000 troops in Africa, down from more than 5,000 two years ago.

France has also been accused of utilising former colonies to prop up corrupt regimes or dictators for personal gain. The practice itself is dubbed as Françafrique by some observers. According to the New York Times,56 African countries are growing concerned about the persistent influence of their former colonial power, France, decades after obtaining independence. Some activist groups are working to have the French presence removed from their nations. Many Africans want France to pull its businesses, embassies, and military out of their country. The article outlines a growing sentiment among several African states to re-establish ties with France and diminish its influence in their affairs. Furthermore, French enterprises and interests typically obtain preferential treatment in these countries' public procurement and bidding processes [57].

However, it is crucial to note that France's influence in Africa has been dwindling recently. African countries are increasingly seeking other global powers for economic and political cooperation, such as China and Russia. In several former colonies, anti-French sentiment has grown, resulting in rallies and attacks on French businesses[58]. As a result, France has been under pressure to abandon its postcolonial tradition of Françafrique and allow for more economic and political sovereignty in its former African colonies[59]. Thus, while France has enormous influence in Africa, its domination is not as strong as it once was. The future of this partnership is dependent on several circumstances, including Africa's economic development, China's rising, and France's changing political landscape.[60]

Affected Economies

France's relationship with its former colonies has an impact on their economies in a variety of ways. As we have already said, the CFA franc, a currency used in 14 former French colonies in West and Central Africa pegged to the euro and guaranteed by the French treasury, is one key component. This agreement mandates African countries to keep a portion of their foreign exchange reserves in France, limiting their economic sovereignty and sustaining neocolonialism[61]. Critics say that the fixed exchange rate of the CFA franc hurts exporting enterprises' competitiveness and disadvantages domestic producers[62].

Furthermore, French enterprises and interests frequently obtain preferential treatment in these countries' public procurement and bidding processes[63]. African countries have lost billions of dollars in revenue as a result of having to sell their natural resources to French corporations at below-market prices[64].

To summarise, French ties with former colonies impacted their economies tremendously. The nature of colonisation altered the type of things traded during the colonial era [65]. French trade with its colonies was primarily centred on primary product imports and manufactured goods exports, making the colonies the primary supplier of natural resources and the key market for French exports [66]. European settlements in French colonies increased trade between France and those colonies, especially in terms of raw material imports and manufactured goods exports [67]. However, there was no evidence of the impact of European settlers on trade in non-French colonies [68]. Trade between former French colonies and France decreased following independence, but trade with the rest of the globe increased [69].

Broader Geopolitical Context

While the above factors certainly play a role, it is crucial to situate them within a broader geopolitical context:

1. Economic and Military Ties: France's long-standing economic interests and military actions in the four nations where French influence has been disrupted as a result of a coup remain significant components in the relationship dynamics. [70].

2. Internal Politics: Domestic problems such as governance challenges, economic inequality, and civil instability also impact these countries' diplomatic stances towards France [71].

As a result, while Macron's domestic policies, notably his perceived affinity with far-right views, may impact the perceptions and attitudes of African countries, particularly those with a significant Muslim population, they are just one aspect in a complicated geopolitical matrix. Understanding the interaction of internal, historical, and global elements is critical for developing informed diplomatic tactics and promoting mutual respect in Franco-African relations.

THOSE WHO MADE FRANCE-AFRIQUE

Here is a list of French Presidents who were instrumental in establishing and developing the "Françafrique" policy:

Charles de Gaulle (1959-1969)

De Gaulle is considered the father of the Françafrique policy, having led Free France during WWII and then as President of the Fifth Republic. During his rule, many African countries gained independence from France. De Gaulle and his African advisor, Jacques Foccart, did, however, develop a network of cooperation agreements with these newly independent nations, particularly in the areas of military, economic, and political collaboration. These connections frequently went beyond state-to-state meetings and included covert talks and operations.

De Gaulle's Vision and Strategic Interests

When Charles de Gaulle took office in 1958, he began a quick pace of decolonisation. Despite the formal termination of colonial ties, France's geopolitical and economic interests in the region remained strong. Instead, where French influence remained, a system of neocolonialism arose.

Strategic Interests: Africa was viewed as a battleground against communism throughout the Cold War. De Gaulle sought to ensure that France's former colonies did not align with the Soviet bloc in order to position France as an independent power[72].

Economic Interests: Africa was critical to France's economic requirements, particularly uranium from Niger, oil from Gabon, and other essential minerals. Controlling these resources was a major problem[73].

The Mechanics of Françafrique

Political Ties: In exchange for loyalty, France frequently supported dictatorial rulers. One famous example is Gabon's Omar Bongo, who governed from 1967 to 2009 and was a key French ally [74].

Economic Relations: The French treasury-backed CFA Franc kept many African economies tethered to France. The currency was chastised for limiting these countries' economic liberty[75].

Military Interventions: France frequently interfered militarily to defend its interests or to support sympathetic regimes. For example, in the 1980s, France intervened in Chad to oppose Libyan expansion[76].

Thus, De Gaulle's African policy was a complicated blend of economic, political, and geopolitical concerns. While it maintained a veneer of independence for African republics, many remained politically, economically, and militarily dependent on France[77].

Georges Pompidou (1969-1974)

Pompidou, who replaced de Gaulle, maintained close ties

with African leaders and ensured the protection of French interests in the continent.

Continuation of the De Gaulle era: Pompidou was widely seen as de Gaulle's political heir, and he mainly maintained, with minor revisions, the Françafrique strategy. He recognised Africa's significance in global geopolitics and France's traditional domains of influence [78].

Economics at the Forefront: Given his banking background, Pompidou firmly focused on economic collaboration. Under his leadership, French corporations expanded their African presence, particularly in the oil, mining, and infrastructure sectors [79].

Political Engagements: Pompidou's tenure saw closer ties with African leaders who were friendly to French interests. However, this was frequently at the expense of backing despotic regimes, leading to allegations of putting economic interests before democratic principles[80].

Military Presence and Cooperation: Pompidou continued France's policy of military interventions to safeguard its interests. Military bases, arms deals, and training missions were a hallmark of Pompidou's African policy, with the French military playing an interventionist role in countries like Chad [81].

Critiques and Controversies: Pompidou came under fire for frequently ignoring human rights violations in favour of economic and geopolitical gains. Critics claimed that this was a continuation of neocolonial tendencies that put French interests ahead of African autonomy[82].

Valéry Giscard d'Estaing (1974-1981)

The emphasis throughout Giscard d'Estaing's leadership was on business partnerships and continuous military excursions in Africa. His associations with some African presidents, such as the Central African Republic's Bokassa, created controversy.

The Context: Giscard d'Estaing assumed the existing structure of Françafrique from his predecessors, De Gaulle and Pompidou. Nevertheless, the postcolonial era was growing increasingly intricate due to the emergence of Soviet influence in Africa and the worldwide economic upheaval seen during the 1970s[83].

The Uranium Affair and Personal Relationships: One of the most notorious incidents linked to Giscard's African policy was the "Uranium Affair," which entailed accusations of procuring uranium from Niger, thereby underscoring the significance of Africa within France's energy plan. Giscard additionally fostered intimate personal relationships with African leaders, most notably Bokassa of the Central African Republic, which generated significant controversy within French politics [84].

Economic Considerations and FDI: During the tenure of President Giscard d'Estaing, there was a concerted effort to augment French foreign direct investment (FDI) in the African continent. The expansion of French enterprises in African countries tended to prioritise French economic interests and the elites inside these nations, thus impeding broader growth[85].

Military Interventions: The maintenance of military

engagement remained a fundamental aspect of France's African policy. Giscard was recognised for his propensity to interfere in support of amicable governments, as exemplified by his involvement in Zaire (presently known as the Democratic Republic of Congo) in 1978, where he assisted rebel forces [86].

Human Rights and Democracy: Despite Giscard's rhetoric on the significance of human rights, his government frequently disregarded instances of abuses, mainly when perpetrated by allies of France. A discernible conflict emerged between advancing French economic and geopolitical objectives and preserving human rights and democratic principles [87]. The choice was for the former.

François Mitterrand (1981-1995)

Initially, Mitterrand pledged a complete departure from Françafrique's historical practices. During his long tenure, however, France maintained its military engagements in Africa and close, sometimes contentious, contacts with African leaders.

If the France-Afrique policy was mainly made by the French conservative right (Gaullist), what was the impact of the Socialists when they accessed power with Francois Mitterrand?

The France-Afrique policy under François Mitterrand underwent several alterations, but the essential objectives of retaining French influence in Africa remained. Mitterrand, the French President from 1981 to 1995, initially promised a significant shift in French African policy to abandon neo-colonial practices and focus on democratisation [88]. He made public financial and material aid from the French state conditional on African countries' democratisation.

Some researchers evaluating the Mitterand era noted developments in France-Africa ties, such as consistent policy towards Africa, adaptation to unique situations, and a widening disparity between French commercial interests and development aid [89]. Furthermore, there was a reform process of the institutions creating and implementing African policy that was ineffective and inconsistent [90].

The fall of the Berlin Wall on November 9, 1989, was a sign of the winds of change blowing through Eastern Europe. Several countries undertook major democratic reforms, marking a historic break with the communist era. Taking advantage of the 16th summit of the heads of state of Africa and France, which took place in La Baule from June 19 to 21, 1990, French President François Mitterrand delivered a speech in which he invited African countries to follow this movement. Establishing a direct link between democracy and development, this speech marked a change in approach for France, which "will link all its efforts to the efforts that will be made to move towards greater freedom."[91] Mitterrand spoke in this regard of the "enthusiastic" aid that his government would grant to those who would bravely take the step of multipartyism, as many African countries were still operating under a single-party system then. The French president, however, defended himself against accusations of interference in the internal affairs of the conference participants, recalling that "this form of colonialism that would consist of constantly lecturing African states and their leaders is a form of colonialism as perverse as any other"[92].

However, an assessment of the data reveals that adequate policy measures have not followed official announcements, and there was general agreement across party lines on the substance of France's African strategy [93]. However, during Mitterrand's presidency, one major shift was cancelling one-third of Sub-Saharan Africa's debt to France, a bold plan for dealing with the crisis[94]. This action was consistent with Mitterrand's emphasis on fostering democracy and development in Africa, although the programme faced problems and criticism.

Jacques Chirac (1995-2007)

Like his predecessors, Chirac emphasised the importance of French-African relations and maintained personal ties with several African presidents.

According to Shin (2010), Chirac's stance towards Africa remained consistent during his 12 years in office, responding to specific conditions such as "cohabitation," the reassertion of US influence in Africa, and the trauma of the Rwandan massacre. There is a widening gap between French economic interests and African development aid. While funding is still primarily directed to former French colonies, commercial interests have shifted to South Africa and Nigeria. The institutions in charge of developing and implementing French African policy were undergoing insufficient transformation, generating concerns about their effectiveness and coherence [95].

Despite changing to specific conditions, Jacques Chirac's persistent stance towards Africa illustrates the need for a consistent approach in foreign policy towards the continent. Chirac's foreign policy towards Africa was based on three main pillars: "the promotion of democracy and human rights, the fight against poverty and underdevelopment, and the promotion of peace and security"[96]. Focusing on economic development and cooperation with African countries also characterised Chirac's foreign policy towards Africa.[97]

Chirac's foreign policy towards Africa was not without controversy. Critics have accused Chirac of supporting authoritarian regimes in Africa, such as that of President Omar Bongo of Gabon[98]. However, Chirac's foreign policy towards Africa significantly shifted from France's traditional "Françafrique" policy[99]. Yet, the widening disparity between French economic interests and African development aid underscores the need for a more balanced approach that combines business interests with aid distribution. The unfinished reform process of the institutions in charge of developing and implementing African policy raises questions about the effectiveness and consistency of French policy towards Africa. This necessitates a comprehensive and successful reform process for better policy coordination and implementation [100].

Nicolas Sarkozy (2007-2012)

Sarkozy sought to redefine and modernise France's connection with Africa, breaking away from the traditional Françafrique links. However, while the rhetoric has changed, many fundamental processes have not. The result is rather catastrophic.

Uncertainty, inconsistency, and confusion characterise Sarkozy's African strategy. There was disagreement regarding whether his approach to Africa was discontinuous or continuous [101]. While he substantially changed France's engagement in Sub-Saharan Africa by lowering military deployment, military intervention in crises continued, as the French military has been involved in three distinct crises — in Côte d'Ivoire, Chad, and the West African Sahel [102]. Sarkozy did not abandon historical practices of backing autocratic dictators, and Africa retained a special role in French diplomacy [103]. The Libyan instance showed the necessity for a clean break with France's neocolonial relations with black Africa, although policy towards black Africa south of the Sahara remained unchanged [104]. Sarkozy, welcomed Colonel Muammar Ghadafi on a state visit in December 2007, even permitting the Libyan commander to set up his bedouin tent on the grounds of the Elysée Palace. A few years later, Sarkozy was in the forefront of the NATO-led campaign against Ghadafi. This abrupt shift in stance was not due to the urgency of the humanitarian situation in Libya, as then stated. That was only the smoke screen that permitted the violent removel and killing of Ghadafi, whose money favourised the election of Sarkozy, as we will learn years later. The

NATO operation also responded to Ghadafi's commitment to fund an African currency to replace the CFA, endangering the entire France-Afrique system. That was not Ghadafi's unforgivable "mistake". Furthermore, under Sarkozy, France was taken off guard by the speed with which the revolutions in Tunisia and Egypt unfolded. Sarkozy's disastrous approach likely marked the beginning of the fraying of ties between France and Africa. The failure of French troops to effectively eliminate the threat of Islamic terrorists in the Sahel region caused unrest and political shifts in African governments, resulting in the establishment of regimes oriented towards Moscow.

François Hollande (2012-2017)

He encountered issues due to the France-Afrique heritage but worked to build more balanced and transparent relationships with African states.

Security, collaboration, and trade were central to Francois Hollande's African policy. Since 2012, he has prioritised French initiatives in Africa, particularly Mali [105]. Hollande promised to break with the unacceptable practices of the past and made initial decisions that pointed towards change in French Africa policy. He did not have links to the networks of la Francafrique and appointed advisors with different backgrounds and experiences. Hollande also emphasised the need for economic and trade ties with African regional organisations such as the Economic Community of West African

States [106]. However, promises of less military participation were not realised, as French forces remained active in numerous conflicts in Sub-Saharan Africa [107]. Hollande's strategy did not depart from previous practises of supporting undemocratic dictators, nor did it remove Africa's unique standing in French diplomacy [108]. According to Paul Balta, French strategy towards North Africa was typified by a lack of a comprehensive approach to the Maghreb in its horizontal dimension[109]. Instead, France pursued bilateral operations in the vertical sense with each of the Maghrib states, with little regard for the connections that had developed between them since their independence. It wasn't until 1985, for the first time since decolonisation, that the Quai d'Orsay (Ministry of Foreign Affairs) gathered its ambassadors to the Maghreb capitals in Paris on October 7 and 8 to compare views and lay the groundwork for an areawide, coordinated policy.[110]

Overall, compared to past French administrations, Hollande's African strategy showed continuity and change [111].

Emmanuel Macron (2017-)

The complex sociopolitical dynamics developing in France under President Macron's leadership, notably his perceived affinity with far-right agendas, send waves worldwide. The issue arises from France's profound colonial past and extensive ties in Africa: Has Macron's domestic policy impacted France's image and connections overseas, particularly in Mali, Burkina Faso, Niger, and Gabon?

Courting the Far Right: Macron's presidency has been characterised by efforts to court far-right voters who formerly supported Marine Le Pen's National Front (now the National Rally). Macron's ascension to power was aided by the collapse of the existing political system and the rise of anti-establishment populist rivals, allowing him to appeal to a broader audience beyond the left-right cleavage [112].On the other hand, Marine Le Pen's electoral support has expanded dramatically, with her party growing significantly in electoral support and rebranding itself as the Rassemblement National [113]. Le Pen's success can be ascribed to using a "de-demonisation" approach to soften the party's image and broaden its electoral base [114].

Macron has attempted to balance responsiveness and accountability in response to the far-right challenge, focusing on technocratic competence as a legitimation tool [115]. Overall, Macron's presidency has been characterised by efforts to meet the concerns of far-right voters, while Le Pen has successfully grown the power and appeal of her party [116]. While considered a tool for broadening his electoral base, this political tactic has raised worries, particularly about immigration and integration issues.

Perceptions of Anti-Muslim Policies: Macron's perceived position on Islam and Muslims in France is central to the debate. Many have seen problematic policies such as the 'Separatism Law' as an attempt to manage and control France's Muslim population [117]. Such legislative actions and public pronouncements have contributed to the view of Macron's presidency as openly anti-Muslim and anti-immigrant [118]. These policies and attitudes in France will harm many African countries, North Africa included [119]. Given their colonial history, many African nations are susceptible to any hint of discrimination or bigotry emerging from their former colonisers. The communal memory of subjugation and the liberation struggle is indelible in the national psyche[120].

France Dégage: Macron's policy strained diplomatic relations with Tunisia, Algeria, Morocco and several Sub-Saharan countries. African leaders, mindful of home sentiments and public opinion, felt forced to take positions that appeared to confront or oppose alleged neocolonial overtures [121]. The call for France to " dégage " is emblematic of a broader societal desire for genuine sovereignty and freedom from outside intrusion or influence [122]. Ironically, an identical call was made against Ben Ali in Tunisia during the 2011 protests that led to his ouster. Many French people should have been surprised to hear Africans repeat the same " dégage " to France under Macron's system! The call for France to "degage" - meaning "get out" or "leave" - emerged in Senegal in 2018 as part of a major grassroots movement called "France Degage." This movement focused on disengaging from the CFA franc, a currency used by 14 mainly former French colonies in Sub-Saharan Africa, which is seen as a symbol of continued French influence in the region[123].

In Senegal, anti-French sentiment emerged, with demonstrations against chronic inequality, government corruption, and stringent coronavirus prohibitions. French-owned businesses were targeted during these rallies, showing discontent towards the previous colonial authority. The protests underscore Senegal's difficult relationship with France, with some commentators attributing anti-French sentiment to the "Franceafrique" system [124].

Following the July 2023 coup, there was a cry in Niger for France to "dégage" [125]. Similarly, during the October 2022 coup in Burkina Faso, supporters of the coup attacked the French embassy in the capital, Ouagadougou[126]. In Mali, there has been debate concerning French colonial plans and their impact on the country. The plea for independence from outside interference is timely in light of Mali's situation and the French military's involvement [127].

Anti-French sentiments have grown in Mali, with protests chanting "bas la France" (down with France) and "France dégage" [128]. These calls for France to leave reflect a broader societal desire for genuine sovereignty and freedom from outside intrusion or influence, particularly from France, which maintains a significant presence in these countries through troops, businesses, and the use of French as an official language.

FRANCE-AFRIQUE IN AGONY

The influence of France in military affairs and maintenance of dominance in business has been a key cog of the Macron agenda. Unlike other former colonial powers, France still has military bases in Côte d'Ivoire, Senegal and Gabon [129]. However, the recent coups in four countries, during Macron's presidency, have shown that France's influence is waning. The perpetrators of the coups have cited the over-whelming influence of France and its president, Emmanuel Macron, in their affairs as one of their motivations[130].

Macron's African policy has been criticised even by French senators who argue that it has failed and led to anti-French sentiment in Africa[131]. Macron received a letter from over 100 senators across France's political spectrum. The signatories bemoaned the Republic's recent "failures and setbacks" in Africa policy and urged the president to reconsider French policy on the continent. Following the rejection of France by Mali, the Central African Republic, Burkina Faso, and, most recently, Niger, the cross-party group warned that more trouble could be on the way in the Ivory Coast and Senegal, where anti-French sentiment is growing. Then there's North Africa, where relations with Morocco and Tunisia have deteriorated and, in the case of Algeria, have become hostile[132].The senators also highlight that the influence of France in Africa has been replaced by the military presence of Russia (Russafrique), the economic influence of China (Chinafrique), and the diplomatic influence of the United States (Americafrique). Despite Macron's efforts to reset France's relationship with Africa, the situation in these countries indicates that there are still significant challenges to overcome.

Unravelling the Franco-African Nexus

What fundamental forces inherent in the Franco-African dynamic may have precipitated such political upheavals? The story becomes even more intriguing when we contrast this with the relative stability of English-speaking countries like Nigeria.

France's Historical and Neo-colonial Footprint

The revolts against France originated in the rich tapestry of France's colonial history in Africa. Following the formal end of colonialism, French influence remained through an elaborate network of military, economic, and diplomatic ties known as "Françafrique," which refers to the military-political phenomenon of French influence and neocolonialism in Africa. Over time, the perception of French policy in Africa has shifted from apologetic to critical, with increasing scrutiny on the concept of Françafrique[133].The French establishment has become more cautious in discussing the actions of politicians and military personnel in Africa, as high-profile revelations and lawsuits have made it a risky topic for French politicians [134]. The corruption ties between French political elites and African states have been a significant aspect of Françafrique, with the French government using legal and illegal methods to defend its regional interests [135]. This has led to client-states forming with corrupt power elites, providing French companies access to strategic resources and control over political parties[136]. The influence of corrupt African leaders on the French political class has also been a concern [137].

Regarding security, traditional approaches focused on military threats have limited relevance in Africa, with the continent facing poverty and human security challenges.

This post-colonial entanglement, known as 'Françafrique,' is characterised by:

1. Economic Leverage: France's control of essential businesses in these countries, particularly resources such as oil and uranium, has been criticised as neocolonialist[138].

2. Military Presence: France's military incursions, particularly in the Sahel region under the guise of counter-terrorism, have fueled resentment and fueled views of foreign meddling[139].

3. Political Influence: Accusations that France handpicks friendly administrations and thereby meddles in domestic politics have long circulated in these countries' political corridors[140].

Socio-Political Reverberations: A Closer Look

The political ecosystems of Mali, Burkina Faso, Niger, and Gabon, while distinct, share several characteristics. Chronic governance challenges, corruption, and a swelling youth demographic exacerbated by unemployment and a lack of tangible possibilities are among them[141]. France's influence, frequently regarded as an impediment to genuine reform, becomes a lightning rod for public resentment.

Comparison with Anglophone Africa: A Contrast

The postcolonial period in Africa was fraught with coups and political upheavals as newly independent states wrestled with the legacy of colonialism and the problems of nation-building. While some coups openly targeted French interests, particularly in its former West African colonies, the British colonial legacy in Africa differed in various ways. We must emphasise that nothing like Mali, Burkina Faso, Niger and Gabon occurred in the former British African colonies. Why, might one ask, countries like Nigeria, steeped in British colonial history, not exhibited similar upheavals against their erstwhile colonisers?

Several factors may help us understand the differences. They are as follows:

1. Distinct Colonial Legacies: The British and French colonial legacies differ fundamentally. Under indirect rule, the British permitted local leaders to retain influence, resulting in a more subtle combination of colonial and native organisations [142]. In the British system, local rulers and institutions were frequently co-opted into the colonial administrative machinery. Decolonisation frequently resulted in less centralised and more diverse systems than in many French colonies[143].

2. Economic Dynamics: While Nigeria has expanded its commercial relations beyond its former coloniser, the aforementioned countries remain economically connected to France[144].

3. Regional Stability Factors: Despite its issues, Nigeria benefits from a robust civil society and media, which have historically played critical roles in balancing power dynamics and guaranteeing accountability[145].

4. Postcolonial Coups in former British Colonies: Several countries that were previously under British authority, including Nigeria, Ghana, Uganda, and Sierra Leone, had coups. However, rather than a direct targeting of British interests, these coups were frequently motivated by internal politics, ethnic tensions, economic crises, or regional dynamics[146].

5. Specific Instances:

- **Ghana (1966):** Kwame Nkrumah, Ghana's first president, was deposed in a military coup while on a state visit to China. While Nkrumah was a staunch Pan-Africanist who opposed neocolonialism, the principal grounds of the coup were internal: economic downturns, claims of corruption, and accusations of growing dictatorial control. Although Nkrumah accused the United States and Britain of involvement in the coup, direct evidence is scarce and debated[147].
- **Uganda (1971):** General Idi Amin deposed President Milton Obote in a coup. While Amin's unstable leadership weakened British-Ugandan relations, the coup itself was not explicitly directed against British interests.
- **Nigeria** has had several coups and counter-coups since independence. Internal causes such as ethnic tensions

between the Hausa-Fulani, Igbo, and Yoruba communities, corruption, and governance concerns fueled the coups in Nigeria. The primary goal of these coups was not British interests [148].

6. Contrast with Françafrique: The coups aimed at French interests in Mali, Burkina Faso, Niger, and Gabon were tightly entwined with the Françafrique networks, which established complicated postwar relationships between France and its former colonies. Britain, on the other hand, did not retain such an open and direct web of neocolonial ties with its former colonies, making anti-British coups less common.

To summarise, the latest revolts in Francophone African nations are simmering tensions rooted in complex past and modern neocolonial activities. The dramatic contrast with Anglophone countries emphasises the Franco-African relationship's features. A thorough understanding of these sociopolitical dynamics is essential to traverse this landscape and even predict future upheavals.

Factor X: Islam?

Mali, Burkina Faso, Niger and Gabon. Four countries revolted recently against France. Three of them are Muslim-majority nations. Only Gabon has about 13% of Muslims. Does the Muslim factor play a role in the revolt against France?

The short answer is: No. We did not find evidence linking

the coups to any Islamist group or Muslim community. The "France Degage" has no religious connotation.

The Sahel area of Africa, encompassing nations such as Mali, Niger, Burkina Faso, and Chad, has been a focal point for political instability and violence. The region, also characterised by severe poverty, is a conflict zone, hosting a multitude of violent armed factions such as Boko Haram, the Islamic State in West Africa Province (ISWAP), and Jama'at Nusrat al-Islam wal-Muslimin (JNIM). "Over the past decade, the Sahel, a vast semiarid region of western and north-central Africa, has become a tangle of transnational terrorist groups, including the Islamic State in the Greater Sahara, Boko Haram and Jama'at Nusrat al-Islam wal-Muslimin[149]."

The Institute for Economics and Peace (IEP) has identified the Sahel region as the emerging focal point of terrorism, as stated in the Global Terrorism Index 2022[150]. The report underscores the multifaceted challenges confronting the Sahel region, encompassing social, economic, political, and security dimensions. The aforementioned obstacles have had a detrimental impact on establishing the requisite circumstances for attaining positive peace, hence perpetuating a recurring pattern of violence and susceptibility. The lack of capacity exhibited by various governments in the Sahel region to deliver adequate security measures has catalysed the persistence of terrorist organisations, thereby leading to a significant escalation in the number of fatalities resulting from acts of terrorism, which has multiplied by a factor of ten during the period spanning from 2007 to 2021[151].

The escalating *anti-French* attitude has emerged as a notable contributing factor to the recent upheavals in the Sahel region. The *recollection of French colonialism* in the Sahel region persists, marked by its violent military operations, coerced labour practices, suppression of dissent, and deliberate eradication of cultural heritage. Recent disappointments and perceived failures by France in the region have further fostered scepticism and hatred against the former colonial power[152].

In the case of Mali, the government extended an invitation to France in 2012 to assist in addressing the security issue prevailing in the northern region. Nevertheless, although the deployment of a substantial number of military personnel as part of Operation Barkhane, there was no discernible enhancement in the overall security conditions. However, there was an increase in the influence of armed organisations, resulting in regular attacks targeting civilians. The aforementioned circumstances escalated suspicions and animosity towards France, ultimately resulting in the expulsion of the French ambassador in the year 2022[153].

In 2022, "The Economist" explained the French failure in the Sahel, admitting that it was responsible for the coups that occurred in Mali and Burkina Faso[154]. The military intervention conducted by France in the Sahel region, referred to as "Operation Barkhane," originally demonstrated efficacy in impeding the progress of jihadist factions within Mali. Nevertheless, these groups have since experienced a significant increase in their power and have expanded their influence to several other nations within the vicinity. In spite of France's diligent endeavours to mitigate their impact, there has been a substantial escalation in the number of injuries and individuals who have been displaced. The region has experienced increased destabilisation, resulting in political turbulence and the occurrence of coups in Mali and Burkina Faso. The popularity of France has experienced a deterioration, as evidenced by the expression of resentment and suspicion against French soldiers by a significant number of local individuals. Russian mercenaries have been sent as a substitute for French military personnel. In light of France's potential exit, it is imperative to recognise that although they successfully averted the collapse of Bamako in 2013, their efforts to suppress the insurgency and garner support from the indigenous populace have been ineffective [155].

Following a military coup in Niger, the individuals responsible for the coup rapidly attributed the country's challenges to France, asserting that it had been instrumental in "destabilising the nation."

The initial finding derived from the research above suggests that the decline of France's power in the Sahel region can primarily be ascribed to its predominately militaristic approach, which proved inadequate in effectively addressing the root causes of conflict.

The second observation pertains to the predominantly Muslim countries of Mali, Burkina Faso, and Niger. The uprisings against France in these regions are primarily driven by historical grievances, perceived neocolonialism, and recent political and military setbacks rather than being motivated solely by religious factors. Gabon, which has a comparatively smaller Muslim population, did not emerge as a prominent focal point within the discussed dynamics.

CHAPTER 5

Geopolitical Factors

Who Profits From the Anti-French Coups?

The occurrence of a succession of anti-French coups in Mali, Burkina Faso, Niger, and Gabon during the early 2020s serves as a reflection of the evolving geopolitical landscape in Africa. France, a former colonial power, is currently striving to uphold its influence in these regions. However, it faces competition from other prominent global powers such as the United States, Russia, and China[156]. When evaluating the prospective beneficiaries of the coups, it is imperative to comprehend the interests and involvements of these powers in the region.

1-The United States :

The United States of America has historically focused primarily on West and Central Africa for counterterrorism efforts, peacekeeping missions, and advancing democratic governance[157]. The United States has provided military training and equipment to many nations, such as Mali, Niger, and Burkina Faso, through the Africa Command (AFRICOM).

Profits: The potential benefits for the United States could arise from the coups if the newly established regimes demonstrate a greater willingness to engage in American security cooperation or prioritise American corporate interests, which they may do if given guarantees involving economic and financial backing and political and military support and protection. But this will happen only if mutual trust exists.

2- China:

China's engagement with the African continent is primarily driven by its Belt and Road Initiative (BRI), the pursuit of natural resource acquisition, and the desire to enhance its political sway. China has emerged as the primary trading partner for Africa, assuming a prominent role in developing infrastructure and mining industries [158]. China has been actively increasing its sphere of influence in Africa, with a specific focus on West Africa, where the influence of France is diminishing. Beijing has been seeking to establish a reciprocal relationship between military procurement and political influence, leveraging its economic supremacy in the area to further its involvement in security matters. According to "France 24," China is increasing its influence in West Africa as France's declines[159]. China's entry into the West African arms market represents a strategic shift for a country that has traditionally focused its weapons sales on other African regions. Norinco, China's largest weapons manufacturer, has launched a new sales office in Senegal and aims to open operations in Mali and the Ivory Coast, where it already sells guns. Senegal, the Ivory Coast, and Mali are all French-speaking countries that, as former colonies, traditionally fell under France's sphere of influence. France remains the largest weaponry supplier in Senegal and Ivory Coast[160]. China's trust in West Africa is growing despite its comparatively modest engagement compared to other continent sections [161]. According to "China Global South," China has surpassed France to become the most significant economic partner of most former French colonies in Africa, notably those in the Franc Zone that use the CFA Franc currency [162].

3. Russia:

In recent years, Russia's engagement in Africa has seen a resurgence, mainly through private military organisations such as the Wagner Group. Russia's principal objectives are to secure rich mining contracts and to enhance its geopolitical influence [163]. Russian weaponry sales and ties to the Wagner military firm, directly subsidised by the Russian government, have been linked to Niger, Sudan, Burkina Faso, and Mali coups[164]. Following the coup, demonstrators in Niger chanted pro-Russian and anti-Western, mainly anti-French, chants[165]. Russia's military involvement in Africa has provided the Kremlin a low-cost means of gaining political and economic influence[166].

If the coups make administrations more receptive to

Russian aspirations, Moscow gains significantly. There have already been indications of rising Russian private military contractors in Mali and other countries [167]. Furthermore, Russia may perceive these coups as a way to weaken France's influence.

In summary, Russia and China appear to be the most likely global powers to profit from the anti-French coups in Mali, Burkina Faso, Niger, and Gabon. These countries could leverage the situation to expand their influence in Africa and establish new alliances.

While all three powers have interests in the region, Russia is the most immediate beneficiary, given its active efforts to challenge French influence. The USA and China have interests in stability and may adapt to changes as they come, but neither would be likely to promote coups actively. It's essential to remember that while these geopolitical factors play a significant role, domestic issues within each country also significantly influence political developments.

CHAPTER 6

Conclusion and Key Findings

Historical connections, economic interdependencies, and geopolitical factors characterise the complex relationship between France and its former African colonies. The ongoing influence exerted by France is being met with an increasing sentiment of opposition in Africa, resulting in the emergence of grassroots movements and political upheavals. The trajectory of this connection will be influenced by both domestic processes within African nations and wider geopolitical considerations.

The following is a summary of the paper's main findings:

1. Historical Context: The occurrence of military coups in Africa emerged as a recurrent phenomenon subsequent to the initial coup d'état in Egypt in 1952. Since then, Africa has experienced more than 200 recorded coup attempts, with a success rate above 40% since 1958.

2. Variables Influencing Military Coups: This study highlights various variables that contribute to the prevalence of military coups in Africa. These elements encompass the historical legacy of colonialism, the establishment of arbitrary colonial borders, ethnic heterogeneity, economic limitations, the absence of democratic customs, and the influence of Cold War politics.

3. Geographical Distribution: The prevalence of military coups has recently been higher in West Africa, the central region for coup occurrences. Nevertheless, instances of coups d'état have taken place in diverse places of Africa, encompassing a minimum of 45 out of the 54 states on the African continent, since these countries have encountered at least one endeavour to overthrow their governments since the year 1950.

4. Persistent Instability: Despite the observable trajectory towards democratisation in Africa since 1990, the region remains plagued by a persistent prevalence of military interventions and coup plots, significantly contributing to the perpetuation of political instability.

5. France's role: The study challenges France's involvement in African coups and the anti-French attitude at some of these events. This study investigates the historical actions of France in Africa and their consequential influence on the political dynamics of the continent.

6. Geopolitical Factors: The study considers how other world powers, such as the USA, China, and Russia, interact with African coups and whether they stand to gain from the instability in African nations.

The present study underscores the complex nature of the variables contributing to military coups in Africa, underscoring the imperative of adopting a multidisciplinary framework to comprehend this phenomenon systematically. Furthermore, this phenomenon prompts significant inquiries into the influence exerted by foreign entities, notably France, on African political dynamics and the manifestation of anti-French sentiment in the context of coup d'états.

Notes

1.   ^ Souaré, Issaka K. "The African Union as a Norm Entrepreneur on Military Coups d'État in Africa (1952-2012): An Empirical Assessment." The Journal of Modern African Studies 52, no. 1 (2014): 69–94. https://www.jstor.org/stable/43302097
2.   ^ AJLabs. "Mapping Africa's Coups d'Etat across the Years." www.aljazeera.com, August 30, 2023. https://tinyurl.com/msj6av7f
3.   ^ McGowan, Patrick J. "African Military Coups d'État, 1956 –2001: Frequency, Trends and Distribution." The Journal of Modern African Studies 41, no. 3 (August 26, 2003): 339–70. https://doi.org/10.1017/s0022278x0300435x
4.   ^ Ibid.
5.   ^ Powell, Jonathan M, and Clayton L Thyne. "Global Instances of Coups from 1950 to 2010: A New Dataset." Journal of Peace Research 48, no. 2 (March 2011): 249–59. https://doi.org/10.1177/0022343310397436
6.   ^ Powell, Jonathan, Abigail Reynolds, and Mwita Chacha. "A New Coup Era for Africa?" ACCORD, March 15, 2022. https://tinyurl.com/y2eu524a
    See also: Duzor, Megan, and Brian Williamson. "By the Numbers: Coups in Africa." projects.voanews.com, February 2, 2022. https://projects.voanews.com/african-coups/
7.   ^ Odigbo, Jude, Kingsley Chukwudubem Ezekwelu, and Remi Chukwudi Okeke. "Democracy's Discontent and the Resurgence of Military Coups in Africa." Journal of Contemporary International Relations and Diplomacy 4, no. 1 (July 4, 2023): 644–55. https://doi.org/10.53982/jcird.2023.0401.01-j

8.   ^ Pryce, Daniel K., and Victoria M. Time. "The Role of Coups d'État in Africa: Why Coups Occur and Their Effects on the Populace." International Social Science Journal, April 20, 2023. https://doi.org/10.1111/issj.12428

9.   ^ Akwei, Benjamin, Benjamin A Machar, and Phiwokuhle Mnyandu. "'Debris' of Coups D'état: Electoral Democracy, Election Violence, Political Vigilantism, and Elections Securitizations in Africa." South Asian Research Journal of Humanities and Social Sciences 5, no. 03 (May 20, 2023): 65–75. https://doi.org/10.36346/sarjhss.2023.v05i03.006

10.   ^ Okon, Enoch Ndem. "WHY MILITARY COUPS ARE BACK in AFRICA." Revista Brasileira de Estudos Africanos 7, no. 14 (December 13, 2022). https://doi.org/10.22456/2448-3923.123042

11.   ^ F.C., Chilaka, and Peter T.O. "Resurgence of Military Coups in West Africa: Implications for ECOWAS." African Journal of Social Sciences and Humanities Research 5, no. 2 (May 19, 2022): 52–64. https://doi.org/10.52589/ajsshr-w9f5vaxe

12.   ^ Collier, Paul, and Anke Hoeffler. "Coup Traps: Why Does Africa Have So Many Coups D'état?" Centre for the Study of African Economies, Department of Economics, University of Oxford, September 1, 2005, 1–28.

13.   ^ Rodney, Walter. How Europe Underdeveloped Africa. 1972. Reprint, London; New York: Verso, 2018.

14.   ^ Herbst, Jeffrey. States and Power in Africa: Comparative Lessons in Authority and Control Comparative Lessons in Authority and Control. Princeton, Nj Princeton University Press, 2000. https://muse.jhu.edu/chapter/1434407

15.   ^ Collier, Paul. The Bottom Billion: Why the Poorest Countries Are Failing and What Can Be Done about It. Oxford: Oxford University Press, 2007.

16.   ^ Meredith, Martin. The Fate of Africa: From the Hopes of Freedom to the Heart of Despair: A History of Fifty Years of Independence. New York: Public Affairs, 2005.

17.   ^ Agüero, Felipe, and Jeffrey Stark. Fault Lines of Democracy in Post-Transition Latin America. Lynne Rienner Publishers, 1998.

18.   ^ Eizenstat, S.E., Lewis, W., & Spence, M. (1998). Agenda for

Africa's Economic Renewal. Peterson Institute for International Economics.

19. ^ Magaloni, B., & Kricheli, R. (2010). Political order and one-party rule. *Annual Review of Political Science, 13*, 123-143.

20. ^ Powell, J. M. (2012). Determinants of the Attempting and Outcome of Coups d'état. Journal of Conflict Resolution, 56 (6), 1017-1040.

21. ^ Chafer, T. (2002). The end of empire in French West Africa: France's successful decolonization? Bloomsbury Academic.

22. ^ Powell, Nathaniel K. "The Flawed Logic behind French Military Interventions in Africa." The Conversation, May 12, 2020. https://tinyurl.com/y9kze6dt.

23. ^ Yates, D.A. (2018). French Military Interventions in Africa. In: Karbo, T., Virk, K. (eds) The Palgrave Handbook of Peacebuilding in Africa. Palgrave Macmillan, Cham. https://doi.org/10.1007/978-3-319-62202-6_22

24. ^ Bon, Daniel, and Karen Mingst. "French Intervention in Africa: Dependency or Decolonization." Africa Today 27, no. 2 (1980): 5–20. https://www.jstor.org/stable/4185920.

25. ^ Huntington, Samuel. "Democracy's Third Wave Can Yugoslavia Survive? Soviet Reaction, Russian Reform Overcoming Underdevelopment," 1991. https://www.ned.org/docs/Samuel-P-Huntington-Democracy-Third-Wave.pdf.

26. ^ Melly, Paul. "Why France Faces so Much Anger in West Africa." BBC News, December 5, 2021, sec. Africa. https://www.bbc.co.uk/news/world-africa-59517501.

27. ^ AFP. "Burkina Junta Chief Says He's against French Policies, Not People." VOA, September 7, 2023. https://tinyurl.com/258a8hua.

28. ^ ACSS. "Understanding Burkina Faso's Latest Coup." Africa Center for Strategic Studies, October 28, 2022. https://tinyurl.com/yry9wtem

29. ^ See: King, Isabelle. "How France Failed Mali: The End of Operation Barkhane." Harvard International Review, January 30, 2023. https://tinyurl.com/ffrbbssv
     Also: Powell, Nathaniel. "Why France Failed in Mali." War on the Rocks, February 21, 2022. https://tinyurl.com/np89sn6x

30.   ^ Akinwotu, Emmanuel. "Mali: Leader of 2020 Coup Takes Power after President's Arrest." The Guardian, May 25, 2021, sec. World news. https://tinyurl.com/2s3fehz6 ; See also: Fornof, Emily, and Emily Cole. "Five Things to Know about Mali's Coup." United States Institute of Peace, August 27, 2020. https://tinyurl.com/y29yhbey

31.   ^ Ajala, Olayinka. "What Caused the Coup in Niger? An Expert Outlines Three Driving Factors." The Conversation, July 31, 2023. https://tinyurl.com/mr46hmwp

32.   ^ Toosi, Nahal, and Clea Caulcutt. "France, U.S. Relations Grow Tense over Niger Coup." POLITICO, August 18, 2023. https://tinyurl.com/5h7bszrh

33.   ^ Ioanes, Ellen (2023), op.Cit.

34.   ^ Schofield, Hugh. "Macron Looks on as France's Africa Policy Crumbles." BBC News, September 1, 2023, sec. Europe. https://tinyurl.com/3f3zz7mn

35.   ^ Camut, Nicolas. "Macron Lays out 'New Era' for France's Reduced Presence in Africa." POLITICO, February 27, 2023. https://tinyurl.com/yubzzaby

36.   ^ Noubel, Filip. "'Françafrique': A Term for a Contested Reality in Franco-African Relations." Global Voices, February 5, 2020. https://tinyurl.com/2s4xennb.

37.   ^ Diop, Boubacar Boris . "Françafrique: A Brief History of a Scandalous Word." New African Magazine, March 23, 2018. https://newafricanmagazine.com/16585/.

38.   ^ Bat, Jean-Pierre. "Le Rôle de La France Après Les Indépendances." Afrique Contemporaine n°235, no. 3 (March 15, 2011): 43–52. https://doi.org/10.3917/afco.235.0043.

    Also: Turpin, Frédéric. "Jacques Foccart et Le RPF En Afrique Noire, Sous La Ive République." Les Cahiers Du Centre de Recherches Historiques, no. 30 (October 30, 2002). https://doi.org/10.4000/ccrh.572.

39.   ^ Médard, Jean-François. "'La Politique Est Au Bout Du Réseau'. Questions Sur La Méthode Foccart." Les Cahiers Du Centre de Recherches Historiques, no. 30 (October 30, 2002). https://doi.org/10.4000/ccrh.612.

40.   ^ Cohen, Corentin. "Will France's Africa Policy Hold Up?" Carnegie Endowment for International Peace., 2022. https://tinyurl.com/ampnsp4a.

41.   ^ Yates, D.A. (2018); op.Cit.

42.   ^ France Diplomacy - Ministry for Europe and Foreign Affairs. "French Diplomacy in Africa: Global Issues," May 2021. https://tinyurl.com/w54aduf6.

43.   ^ Ibid.

44.   ^ France Diplomacy - Ministry for Europe and Foreign Affairs. "Franc Zone," December 2021. https://tinyurl.com/5z35wffj.

45.   ^ Banque de France. "Africa-France Monetary Cooperation," April 5, 2022. https://tinyurl.com/3c2pxu53.

46.   ^ BCEAO. "CFA Franc | History and Information | June 1, 2016. https://tinyurl.com/yc7a6zj4.

47.   ^ Sylla, Ndongo Samba. "The CFA Franc: French Monetary Imperialism in Africa |." Africa at LSE, July 12, 2017. https://tinyurl.com/mr37vats.

48.   ^ Bryant, Lisa. "France Struggles to Reshape Relations in Africa." VOA, September 6, 2023. https://tinyurl.com/58zbh32z.

49.   ^ Keaten, Jamey, Sam Mednick, and Cara Anna. "France's Waning Influence in Coup-Hit Africa Appears Clear While Few Remember Their Former Colonizer." ABC News, September 4, 2023. https://tinyurl.com/ydk54dnt.

50.   ^ Dite, Chris, Fanny Pigeaud, and Ndongo Samba Sylla. "Africa: How France Continues to Dominate Its Former Colonies in Africa." CADTM, September 14, 2023. https://tinyurl.com/bdddw93x.

51.   ^ Ibid.

52.   ^ Dite, Pigeaud, and Sylla (2023); op. Cit.

53.   ^ Buehler, William. "French Economic Neocolonialism in West and Central Africa." The Phillipian, December 9, 2022. https://tinyurl.com/4zdkcbwk.

54.   ^ Hansen, Andrew. "The French Military in Africa." Council on Foreign Relations, February 8, 2008. https://tinyurl.com/4sud44y3.

55.   ^ Chrisafis, Angelique. "Macron Pledges to Reduce French Military Presence in Africa." The Guardian, February 27, 2023, sec. World news. https://tinyurl.com/y4ypb4s4.

56. ^ Maclean, Ruth. "'Down with France': Former Colonies in Africa Demand a Reset." The New York Times, April 14, 2022, sec. World. https://tinyurl.com/csu2mppm.

57. ^ EU Reporter Correspondent. "France Accused of 'Still Controlling' Some of Its Former Colonies in Africa." EU Reporter, October 13, 2021. https://tinyurl.com/42fy2v9p.

58. ^ Busari, Stephanie. "Gabon Coup Shows How France's Influence on Its Former Territories Is Disintegrating." CNN, September 1, 2023. https://tinyurl.com/4hs488ht.

59. ^ Andjembe Etogho, Elvine Belinda, Sphynx Egbe-Mbah Eben, and Amy L. Dalton. "French Neocolonialism in Africa: Historical Overview and Summary of Current Events." The American Journal of Economics and Sociology 81, no. 5 (November 2022): 829–49. https://doi.org/10.1111/ajes.12493.

60. ^ Benneyworth, I. J. "The Ongoing Relationship between France and Its Former African Colonies." E-International Relations, June 11, 2011. https://tinyurl.com/bd8advts.

61. ^ Dite, Pigeaud, and Sylla (2023), op.Cit.

62. ^ Herrera, Remy. "An Uncompromising Criticism of the CFA Franc." Africa Is a Country, June 22, 2022. https://tinyurl.com/ms86f686.

63. ^ Dite, Chris. "How France Continues to Dominate Its Former Colonies in Africa." jacobin.com, March 29, 2021. https://tinyurl.com/f7m4mxmt.

64. ^ Ndum, Nanji. "The Françafrique Conundrum: A Critical Analysis of France's Influence in Africa." LinkedIn, March 10, 2023. https://tinyurl.com/47jemc53.

65. ^ Neifar, Malika. "Colonial Legacies on Employment: Comparisons between Some Former Anglophone and French Colonies." Review of Economics and Political Science 8, no. 1 (November 18, 2022). https://doi.org/10.1108/reps-06-2022-0038.

66. ^ Kallab, Tania El, ed. "French Colonial Trade Patterns: Facts and Impacts." African Journal of Agricultural and Resource Economics 13, no. 1 (2018). https://doi.org/10.22004/ag.econ.273134.

67. ^ Ibid.

68. ^ El Kallab, Tania, and Cristina Terra. "French Colonial Trade Patterns and European Settlements." Comparative Economic Studies

60, no. 3 (December 21, 2017): 291–331. https://doi.org/10.1057/s41294-017-0040-6.

69.   ^ Lochard, Julie. "Independence and Trade: The Specic Effects of French Colonialism." Post-Print. HAL, February 2, 2012. https://ideas.repec.org/p/hal/journl/hal-01609942.html.

70.   ^ Chafer, Tony. The End of Empire in French West Africa. Berg Publishers, 2002.

71.   ^ Bach, Daniel C. "Inching towards a Country without a State: Prebendalism, Violence and State Betrayal in Nigeria." In BIG AFRICAN STATES. Johannesburg: Wits University Press, 2006.

72.   ^ Connelly, Matthew. "Rethinking the Cold War and Decolonisation: The Grand Strategy of the French Fourth Republic, 1945-1954." Diplomatic History 24.2 (2000): 163-198.

73.   ^ Verschave, François-Xavier. La Françafrique: Le plus long scandale de la République. Stock, 1998.

74.   ^ Chafer, Tony. "The end of the French African empire? France's Africa policy under Chirac." The Journal of Modern African Studies 38.2 (2000): 251-278.

75.   ^ Stasavage, David. "The CFA Franc: French monetary imperialism in Africa." International Organization 53.4 (1999): 733-762.

76.   ^ Heerten, Lasse, and A. Dirk Moses. "The Nigeria–Biafra war: postcolonial conflict and the question of genocide." Journal of Genocide Research 16.2-3 (2014): 169-203.

77.   ^ Smith, Stephen. La guerre des clans: Mobutu, Kabila, et les autres. Calmann-Lévy, 1999.

78.   ^ Cooper, Frederick. "Possibility and Constraint: African Independence in Historical Perspective." Journal of African History 49.2 (2008): 167-196.

79.   ^ Chipman, John. "French Power in Africa." Blackwell Publishers, 1989.

80.   ^ Peemans, Jean-Philippe. "Capital accumulation and transition: The rise of the West." Review (Fernand Braudel Center) (1990): 211-244.

81.   ^ Utley, Rachel. "France and the Chad Crisis: superpower-proxy interventionism in Africa." Review of International Studies 17.2 (1991): 131-148.

82. ^ Martin, Guy. "Continuity and change in Franco-African rela-tions." Journal of Modern African Studies 30.1 (1992): 53-80.

83. ^ Englebert, Pierre. "State Legitimacy and Development in Africa." Lynne Rienner Publishers, 2000.

84. ^ Smith, Stephen. "Nostalgie Bokassa." Politique africaine 34 (1989): 82-88.

85. ^ Bach, Daniel C. "Françafrique: Currents and Ruptures." Politique africaine 99 (2005): 132-148.

86. ^ Utley, (1991), op. Cit.

87. ^ Martin, Guy. "Africa in French International Strategy." Journal of Contemporary African Studies 12.1 (1993): 15-36.

88. ^ Frankel, Glenn. "France Turns Pragmatic toward Africa." Washington Post, December 18, 1984. https://tinyurl.com/bddanshf.

89. ^ "Algeria – France: Normalised Relations." Africa Research Bulletin: Political, Social and Cultural Series 59, no. 12 (January 1, 2023). https://doi.org/10.1111/j.1467-825x.2023.10859.x.

90. ^ Khan, M. Faizullah. "Africa and France: postcolonial cultures, migration, and racism, by Dominic Thomas, Bloomington, Indiana University Press, 2013, Africa Review 8, 1 (2016): 77-79, doi: https://doi.org/10.1080/09744053.2015.1090667

91. ^ Perspective Monde. "Discours Du Président Français François Mitterrand Sur La Démocratisation En Afrique | Evenements | Perspective Monde," June 20, 1990. https://tinyurl.com/3p5buhhn.

92. ^ Ibid.

93. ^ Echikson, William. "Mitterrand in Africa to Tighten Francophone Ties." Christian Science Monitor, May 20, 1982. https://tinyurl.com/2rmkrh48.

94. ^ Greenhouse, Steven, "French Plan to Forgive Africa Debt." The New York Times, June 9, 1988, sec. Business. https://tinyurl.com/2s3t8s5y.

95. ^ Shin, Won Yong. "[PDF] French Foreign Policy towards Africa under Jacques Chirac by Shin, Won Yong · 2287276104 · OA.mg." Oa.mg 3, no. 2 (December 1, 2010): pp 75-89. https://oa.mg/work/2287276104.

96. ^ Siradağ, Abdurrahim. "Understanding French Foreign and Security Policy towards Africa: Pragmatism or Altruism." Afro Eur-

asian Studies 3, no. 1 (June 1, 2014): 100–122. https://tinyurl.com/497y49ka.

97.   ^ Ibid.

98.   ^ Shin, (2010), op. Cit.

99.   ^ Touati, Sylvain. "French Foreign Policy in Africa: Between PRÉ CARRÉ and Multilateralism ." Chatham House. An Africa Programme Briefing Note, February 2007. https://tinyurl.com/2czwzkny.

100.   ^ Shin, (2010), op. Cit.

101.   ^ Cumming, Gordon D. "Nicolas Sarkozy's Africa Policy: Change, Continuity or Confusion?" French Politics 11, no. 1 (March 12, 2013): 24–47. https://doi.org/10.1057/fp.2012.24.

102.   ^ Cumming, G.D. (2013). 'A Piecemeal Approach with No Vision': French Policy Towards Africa under Nicolas Sarkozy. In: Raymond, G.G. (eds) The Sarkozy Presidency. French Politics, Society and Culture Series. Palgrave Macmillan, London. https://doi.org/10.1057/9781137025326_6

103.   ^ Moncrieff, Richard. "French Africa Policy: Sarkozy's Legacy, and Prospects for a Hollande Presidency." South African Journal of International Affairs 19, no. 3 (December 2012): 359–80. https://doi.org/10.1080/10220461.2012.741104.

104.   ^ Filippov, Vasily. "African Policy of France in 2017–2023." Asia and Africa Today, no. 5 (January 1, 2023): 65–65. https://doi.org/10.31857/s032150750025686-6.

105.   ^ Medushevskiy, Nikolay A, and Alisa R Shishkina. "Modern French Policy on the African Continent: Transformations of a Françafrique Model." Journal of Asian and African Studies 57, no. 6 (September 19, 2021): 002190962110462. https://doi.org/10.1177/00219096211046275.

106.   ^ Chafer, Tony. "Hollande and Africa Policy." Modern & Contemporary France 22, no. 4 (October 2, 2014): 513–31. https://doi.org/10.1080/09639489.2014.957966.

107.   ^ Moncrieff (2012), op. Cit.

108.   ^ Balta, Paul. "French Policy in North Africa." Middle East Journal 40, no. 2 (1986): 238–51. https://www.jstor.org/stable/4327308.

109. ^ Ibid.

110. ^ Balta, (1986), op.Cit.

111. ^ Labouret, Henri. "France's Colonial Policy in Africa." African Affairs XXXIX, no. CLIV (January 1940): 22–35. https://doi.org/10.1093/oxfordjournals.afraf.a100972.

112. ^ Vermersch, Lucie Viviane Danielle. "Framing Immigration and National Sovereignty in the French Far-Right: Marine Le Pen's Rhetoric and the Dédiabolisation Strategy." Knowledge UChicago, June 2022. https://knowledge.uchicago.edu/record/3732.

113. ^ Perottino, Michel, and Petra Guasti. "Technocratic Populism à La Française? The Roots and Mechanisms of Emmanuel Macron's Success." Politics and Governance 8, no. 4 (December 17, 2020): 545–55. https://doi.org/10.17645/pag.v8i4.3412.

114. ^ Mayer, Nonna. "From Jean-Marie to Marine Le Pen: Electoral Change on the Far Right." Parliamentary Affairs 66, no. 1 (2013): 160–78. https://doi.org/10.1093/pa/gss071.

115. ^ Startin, Nicholas. "Marine Le Pen, the Rassemblement National and Breaking the 'Glass Ceiling'? The 2022 French Presidential and Parliamentary Elections." Modern & Contemporary France 30, no. 4 (November 11, 2022): 1–17. https://doi.org/10.1080/09639489.2022.2138841.

116. ^ Karawita, Amali. "The Persuasiveness of France's Far-Right Movement: The Case of Marine Le Pen." JURNAL KOMUNIKASI INDONESIA 8, no. 1 (March 1, 2019). https://doi.org/10.7454/jki.v8i1.10399.

117. ^ Cesari, J. (2020). *Securitisation of Islam in Europe*. European View, 19(1), 57-66.

118. ^ Williamson, Lucy. "France Islam: Muslims under Pressure to Sign French Values Charter." BBC News, December 1, 2020, sec. Europe. https://www.bbc.co.uk/news/world-europe-55132098.
      See also: Islam, Shada. "Why Europe's Muslims Are Braced for France's Stint Running the EU Presidency." The Guardian, January 3, 2022, sec. World news. https://tinyurl.com/5n86f9ru.

119. ^ Hird, Alison. "France Slashes Visas for Tunisia, Algeria, Morocco in Row over Illegal Migration." RFI, September 28, 2021. https://tinyurl.com/rttehuv7.

120. ^ Cesari, J. (2020), op. Cit.

121.   ^ Oğurlu, Ebru. "EUROPEAN NEO-COLONIALISM in AF-
RICA." Uluslararası Politik Araştırmalar Dergisi 4, no. 2 (August 30,
2018): 1–21. https://doi.org/10.25272/j.2149-8539.2018.4.2.01.

122.   ^ Burke, Jason. "Macron Seeks African Reset with New View of
France's Troubled History on Continent." The Observer, May 29,
2021, sec. World news. https://tinyurl.com/ycmjff2f.

123.   ^ Thomas-Johnson, Amandla. "Why Is Anti-French Sentiment
Spiking in Senegal Protests?" www.aljazeera.com, March 12, 2021.
https://tinyurl.com/msecxrwx.

124.   ^ Ibid.

125.   ^ France info. "Coup d'Etat Au Niger : Pourquoi La France
a Été Prise Pour Cible Par Des Manifestants," July 31, 2023.
https://tinyurl.com/yt7kpa2f.

126.   ^ Caulcutt, Clea. "French Symbols Targeted after Burkina
Faso Coup." POLITICO, October 2, 2022. https://tinyurl.com/
mvcf7prx.

127.   ^ Kane, Pape Samba. "The French Colonial Designs in Mali." Al
Jazeera, August 22, 2019. https://tinyurl.com/3nc8snff.

128.   ^ France info. "Les Manifestations Anti-Françaises Se Multiplient
Au Mali," January 14, 2020. https://tinyurl.com/yckvch8m.

129.   ^ Gerits, Frank. "France in Africa: Why Macron's Policies Increased Distrust and Anger." The Conversation, September 5, 2023.
https://tinyurl.com/bp5tsfv6

130.   ^ Ibid.

131.   ^ Mortimer, Gavin. "Macron Can't Escape Blame for France's Failures in Africa." The Spectator, August 9, 2023. https://tinyurl.com/
ypxjhux7.

132.   ^ Gerits, (2023); op. Cit.

133.   ^ "AFRICA – FRANCE: 'Committed' to Security." Africa Research Bulletin: Political, Social and Cultural Series 59, no. 7 (August 2022). https://doi.org/10.1111/j.1467-825x.2022.10639.x.

134.   ^ Filippov, Vasily. "The 'Françafrique' Phenomenon as Reflected
in French Historiography." Uchenie Zapiski Instituta Afriki RAN
60, no. 3 (September 7, 2022): 73–87. https://doi.org/10.31132/
2412-5717-2022-60-3-73-87.

135.   ^ Pascal Airault, and Jean-Pierre Bat. Françafrique. Tallandier,
2019.

136. ^ Hough, Peter. "Security in Africa ." In International Security Studies. Routledge, 2020.

137. ^ Filippov, V.R. "Françafrique and Ethics in International Relations." VESTNIK RUDN INTERNATIONAL RELATIONS 17, no. 2 (2017): 402–15. https://doi.org/10.22363/2313-0660-2017-17-2-402-415.

138. ^ Chabal, Patrick, and Jean-Pascal Daloz. Culture Troubles. IB Tauris, 2006.

139. ^ Macgovern, Mike. Making War in Côte D'Ivoire. Chicago: University Of Chicago Press, 2011.

140. ^ Pitcher, Anne, Mary H. Moran, and Michael Johnston. "Rethinking Patrimonialism and Neopatrimonialism in Africa." African Studies Review 52, no. 1 (April 2009): 125–56. https://doi.org/10.1353/arw.0.0163.

141. ^ Bierschenk, Thomas, and Jean-Pierre Olivier de Sardan. "Powers in the Village: Rural Benin between Democratisation and Decentralisation." Africa 73, no. 2 (May 2003): 145–73. https://doi.org/10.3366/afr.2003.73.2.145.

142. ^ Crowder, Michael. Colonial West Africa: Collected Essays. London: Frank Cass, 1978.

143. ^ Lugard, Frederick D. "The Dual Mandate in British Tropical Africa." London: Blackwood, 1922.

144. ^ M. Watts, "Crude Politics: Life and Death on the Nigerian Oil Fields," Niger Delta Economies of Violence Working Papers, Institute of International Studies, University of California, Berkeley, The United States Institute of Peace, Washington, DC, Paper No. 25, 2009.

145. ^ Diamond, Larry. Class, Ethnicity and Democracy in Nigeria : The Failure of the First Republic. London: Palgrave Macmillan UK : Imprint : Palgrave Macmillan, 1988.

146. ^ Decalo, Samuel. "Military Coups and Military Regimes in Africa." Journal of Modern African Studies 11.1 (1973): 105-127.

147. ^ Pinkney, Robert. "Ghana under military rule." Methuen & Co Ltd, 1972.

148. ^ Siollun, Max. "Oil, politics and violence: Nigeria's military coup culture (1966-1976)." New York: Algora Publishing, 2009.

149. ^ Clarke, Colin P. "Opinion | If Your Country Is Falling Apart,

the Wagner Group Will Be There." The New York Times, August 11, 2023, sec. Opinion. https://tinyurl.com/5n6nsx2f.

150.   ^ Vision of Humanity. "Terrorism in the Sahel | Global Terrorism Index 2022." The Global Terrorism Index 2022 produced by Institute for Economics & Peace., April 21, 2022. https://tinyurl.com/y6un4km3.

151.   ^ Ibid.

152.   ^ Aina, Folahanmi. "French Mistakes Helped Create Africa's Coup Belt." www.aljazeera.com, August 17, 2023. https://tinyurl.com/3cbkx47k.

153.   ^ Ibid.

154.   ^ The Economist. "What Have French Forces Achieved in the Sahel?," February 14, 2022. https://tinyurl.com/4uenfkpx.

155.   ^ Ibid.

156.   ^ Tastan , Necva. "Türkiye, Russia, China Could Fill Void Left by France in Africa: Professor." Anadolu Agency , September 14, 2023. https://tinyurl.com/2xfzrcjv.

157.   ^ Carbone, M. (2005). Policy transfer in the European Union: institutions, governance, and the developing world. Development Policy Review, 23(5), 619-637.

158.   ^ Brautigam, D. (2009). The Dragon's Gift: The Real Story of China in Africa. Oxford: Oxford University Press.

159.   ^ Seibt, Sébastian. "Friends at Any Price: China Seeks Allies, Arms Markets in West Africa as French Influence Wanes." France 24, August 26, 2023. https://tinyurl.com/p76d7zxk.

160.   ^ Ibid.

161.   ^ Staden, Cobus van. "China's Growing Influence in West Africa." The China Global South Project, November 10, 2022. https://tinyurl.com/4n9eapn6.

162.   ^ Che, Afa'anwi Ma'abo. "China's Rise in the African Franc Zone and France's Containment Policy." E-International Relations, August 7, 2019. https://tinyurl.com/hjbpvfwv.

163.   ^ Alden, C., & Alves, A. C. (2008). History & identity in the construction of China's Africa policy. *Review of African Political Economy, 35*(115), 43-58.

164.   ^ Blank, Stephen. "The Niger Coup Exposes Russia's Grand

Strategy for Africa." The Hill, August 4, 2023. https://tinyurl.com/24wwj3hd.

165.   ^ Ibid.

166.   ^ Droin, Mathieu, and Tina Dolbaia. "Russia Is Still Progressing in Africa. What's the Limit?" CSIS, August 15, 2023. https://tinyurl.com/4ttkwd4m.

167.   ^ Stronski, P., & Sokolsky, R. (2020). Russia's game in Libya. Carnegie Endowment for International Peace.

References

"AFRICA – FRANCE: 'Committed' to Security." *Africa Research Bulletin: Political, Social and Cultural Series* 59, no. 7 (August 2022). https://doi.org/10.1111/j.1467-825x.2022.10639.x.

Agüero, Felipe, and Jeffrey Stark. *Fault Lines of Democracy in Post-Transition Latin America*. Lynne Rienner Publishers, 1998.

Aina, Folahanmi. "French Mistakes Helped Create Africa's Coup Belt." www.aljazeera.com, August 17, 2023. https://tinyurl.com/3cbkx47k.

AJLabs. "Mapping Africa's Coups D'Etat across the Years." www.aljazeera.com, August 2023. https://tinyurl.com/msj6av7f.

Alden, C., & Alves, A. C. (2008). History & identity in the construction of China's Africa policy. Review of African Political Economy, 35 (115), 43-58.

"Algeria – France: Normalised Relations." *Africa Research Bulletin: Political, Social and Cultural Series* 59, no. 12 (January 1, 2023). https://doi.org/10.1111/j.1467-825x.2023.10859.x.

Bach, Daniel C. "Françafrique: Currents and Ruptures." Politique africaine 99 (2005): 132-148.

Bach, Daniel C. "Inching towards a Country without a State: Prebendalism, Violence and State Betrayal in Nigeria." In *BIG AFRICAN STATES*. Johannesburg : Wits University Press, 2006.

Balta, Paul. "French Policy in North Africa." *Middle East Journal* 40, no. 2 (1986): 238–51. https://www.jstor.org/stable/4327308.

Bat, Jean-Pierre. "Le Rôle de La France Après Les

Indépendances." *Afrique Contemporaine* n°235, no. 3 (March 15, 2011): 43–52. https://doi.org/10.3917/afco.235.0043.

Bierschenk, Thomas, and Jean-Pierre Olivier de Sardan. "Powers in the Village: Rural Benin between Democratisation and Decentralisation." *Africa* 73, no. 2 (May 2003): 145–73. https://doi.org/10.3366/afr.2003.73.2.145.

Blank, Stephen. "The Niger Coup Exposes Russia's Grand Strategy for Africa." The Hill, August 4, 2023. https://tinyurl.com/24wwj3hd.

Brautigam, D. (2009). The Dragon's Gift: The Real Story of China in Africa. Oxford: Oxford University Press.

Burke, Jason. "Macron Seeks African Reset with New View of France's Troubled History on Continent." *The Observer*, May 29, 2021, sec. World news. https://tinyurl.com/ycmjff2f.

Carbone, M. (2005). Policy transfer in the European Union: institutions, governance, and the developing world. Development Policy Review, 23(5), 619-637.

Caulcutt, Clea. "French Symbols Targeted after Burkina Faso Coup." POLITICO, October 2, 2022. https://tinyurl.com/mvcf7prx.

Cesari, Jocelyne. "The Securitisation of Islam in Europe." CEPS, August 26, 2009. https://www.ceps.eu/ceps-publications/securitisation-islam-europe/.

Chabal, Patrick, and Jean-Pascal Daloz. *Culture Troubles*. IB Tauris, 2006.

Chafer, T. (2002). The end of empire in French West Africa: France's successful decolonization? Bloomsbury Academic.

Chafer, Tony. "Hollande and Africa Policy." *Modern & Contemporary France* 22, no. 4 (October 2, 2014): 513–31. https://doi.org/10.1080/09639489.2014.957966.

Chafer, Tony. "The end of the French African empire? France's Africa policy under Chirac." The Journal of Modern African Studies 38.2 (2000): 251-278.

Chipman, John. "French Power in Africa." Blackwell Publishers, 1989.

Connelly, Matthew. "Rethinking the Cold War and Decolonisation: The Grand Strategy of the French Fourth Republic, 1945-1954." Diplomatic History 24.2 (2000): 163-198.

Cooper, Frederick. "Possibility and Constraint: African Independence in Historical Perspective." Journal of African History 49.2 (2008): 167-196.

Crowder, Michael. Colonial West Africa: Collected Essays. London: Frank Cass, 1978.

Cumming, G.D. (2013). 'A Piecemeal Approach with No Vision': French Policy Towards Africa under Nicolas Sarkozy. In: Raymond, G.G. (eds) The Sarkozy Presidency. French Politics, Society and Culture Series. Palgrave Macmillan, London. https://doi.org/10.1057/9781137025326_6

Decalo, Samuel. "Military Coups and Military Regimes in Africa." Journal of Modern African Studies 11.1 (1973): 105-127.

Diamond, Larry. Class, Ethnicity and Democracy in Nigeria : The Failure of the First Republic. London: Palgrave Macmillan UK : Imprint : Palgrave Macmillan, 1988.

Englebert, Pierre. "State Legitimacy and Development in Africa." Lynne Rienner Publishers, 2000.

Heerten, Lasse, and A. Dirk Moses. "The Nigeria–Biafra war: postcolonial conflict and the question of genocide." Journal of Genocide Research 16.2-3 (2014): 169-203.

Khan, M. Faizullah. "Africa and France: postcolonial cultures, migration, and racism, by Dominic Thomas, Bloomington, Indiana University Press, 2013, *Africa Review* 8, 1 (2016): 77-79, doi: https://doi.org/10.1080/09744053.2015.1090667

Lugard, Frederick D. "The Dual Mandate in British Tropical Africa." London: Blackwood, 1922.

Martin, Guy. "Africa in French International Strategy." Journal of Contemporary African Studies 12.1 (1993): 15-36.

M. Watts, "Crude Politics: Life and Death on the Nigerian Oil Fields," Niger Delta Economies of Violence Working Papers, Institute of International Studies, University of California, Berkeley, The United States Institute of Peace, Washington, DC, Paper No. 25, 2009.

Peemans, Jean-Philippe. "Capital accumulation and transition:

The rise of the West." Review (Fernand Braudel Center) (1990): 211-244.

Pinkney, Robert. "Ghana under military rule." Methuen & Co Ltd, 1972.

Powell, J. M. (2012). Determinants of the Attempting and Outcome of Coups d'état. Journal of Conflict Resolution, 56 (6), 1017-1040.

Siollun, Max. "Oil, politics and violence: Nigeria's military coup culture (1966-1976)." New York: Algora Publishing, 2009.

Smith, Stephen. La guerre des clans: Mobutu, Kabila, et les autres. Calmann-Lévy, 1999.

Smith, Stephen. "Nostalgie Bokassa." Politique africaine 34 (1989): 82-88.

Stasavage, David. "The CFA Franc: French monetary imperialism in Africa." International Organization 53.4 (1999): 733-762.

Stronski, P., & Sokolsky, R. (2020). Russia's game in Libya. Carnegie Endowment for International Peace.

———. The End of Empire in French West Africa. Berg Publishers, 2002.

Che, Afa'anwi Ma'abo. "China's Rise in the African Franc Zone and France's Containment Policy." E-International Relations, August 7, 2019. https://tinyurl.com/hjbpvfwv.

CIA World Factbook. "Mali - the World Factbook," September 8, 2023. https://www.cia.gov/the-world-factbook/countries/mali/.

Clarke, Colin P. "Opinion | If Your Country Is Falling Apart, the Wagner Group Will Be There." The New York Times, August 11, 2023, sec. Opinion. https://tinyurl.com/5n6nsx2f.

Cohen, Corentin. "Will France's Africa Policy Hold Up?" Carnegie Endowment for International Peace. , 2022. https://tinyurl.com/ampnsp4a.

Collier, Paul. The Bottom Billion : Why the Poorest Countries Are Failing and What Can Be Done about It. Oxford University Press, 2007.

Cooper, Frederick. Colonialism in Question: Theory, Knowledge, History. Berkeley, California: University of California Press, 2009.

Crowder, Michael. *Colonial West Africa : Collected Essays*. London: Frank Cass, 1978.

Cumming, Gordon D. "Nicolas Sarkozy's Africa Policy: Change, Continuity or Confusion?" *French Politics* 11, no. 1 (March 12, 2013): 24–47. https://doi.org/10.1057/fp.2012.24.

Diamond, Larry. *Class, Ethnicity and Democracy in Nigeria : The Failure of the First Republic*. London: Palgrave Macmillan UK : Imprint : Palgrave Macmillan, 1988.

Diop , Boubacar Boris . "Françafrique: A Brief History of a Scandalous Word." New African Magazine, March 23, 2018. https://newafricanmagazine.com/16585/.

Droin, Mathieu, and Tina Dolbaia. "Russia Is Still Progressing in Africa. What's the Limit?" *CSIS*, August 15, 2023. https://tinyurl.com/4ttkwd4m.

Duzor, Megan, and Brian Williamson. "By the Numbers: Coups in Africa." projects.voanews.com, February 2022. https://projects.voanews.com/african-coups/.

Echikson, William . "Mitterrand in Africa to Tighten Francophone Ties." Christian Science Monitor, May 20, 1982. https://tinyurl.com/2rmkrh48.

Eizenstat, S.E, W Lewis, and M Spence. *Agenda for Africa's Economic Renewal*. Peterson Institute for International Economics., 1998.

Filippov, V.R. "Françafrique and Ethics in International Relations." *VESTNIK RUDN INTERNATIONAL RELATIONS* 17, no. 2 (2017): 402–15. https://doi.org/10.22363/2313-0660-2017-17-2-402-415.

Filippov, Vasily. "The 'Françafrique' Phenomenon as Reflected in French Historiography." *Uchenie Zapiski Instituta Afriki RAN* 60, no. 3 (September 7, 2022): 73–87. https://doi.org/10.31132/2412-5717-2022-60-3-73-87.

Filippov, Vasily . "African Policy of France in 2017–2023." *Asia and Africa Today*, no. 5 (January 1, 2023): 65–65. https://doi.org/10.31857/s032150750025686-6.

France info. "Coup d'Etat Au Niger : Pourquoi La France a Été Prise Pour Cible Par Des Manifestants," July 31, 2023. https://tinyurl.com/yt7kpa2f.

France info. "Les Manifestations Anti-Françaises Se Multiplient Au Mali," January 14, 2020. https://tinyurl.com/yckvch8m.

Frankel, Glenn. "France Turns Pragmatic toward Africa." *Washington Post*, December 18, 1984. https://tinyurl.com/bd-danshf.

Gerits, Frank. "France in Africa: Why Macron's Policies Increased Distrust and Anger." The Conversation, September 5, 2023. https://tinyurl.com/ys6ha2jx.

Greenhouse, Steven, and Special To the New York Times. "French Plan to Forgive Africa Debt." *The New York Times*, June 9, 1988, sec. Business. https://tinyurl.com/2s3t8s5y.

Herbst, Jeffrey. *States and Power in Africa: Comparative Lessons in Authority and Control Comparative Lessons in Authority and Control*. Princeton, Nj Princeton University Press, 2000. https://muse.jhu.edu/chapter/1434407.

Hird, Alison. "France Slashes Visas for Tunisia, Algeria, Morocco in Row over Illegal Migration." RFI, September 28, 2021. https://tinyurl.com/rttehuv7.

Hough, Peter . "Security in Africa ." In *International Security Studies*. Routledge, 2020.

Huntington, Samuel. "Democracy's Third Wave Can Yugoslavia Survive? Soviet Reaction, Russian Reform Overcoming Underdevelopment," 1991. https://www.ned.org/docs/Samuel-P-Huntington-Democracy-Third-Wave.pdf.

Islam, Shada. "Why Europe's Muslims Are Braced for France's Stint Running the EU Presidency." *The Guardian*, January 3, 2022, sec. World news. https://tinyurl.com/5n86f9ru.

Kane, Pape Samba. "The French Colonial Designs in Mali." Al Jazeera, August 22, 2019. https://tinyurl.com/3nc8snff.

Karawita, Amali. "The Persuasiveness of France's Far-Right Movement: The Case of Marine Le Pen." *JURNAL KOMUNIKASI INDONESIA* 8, no. 1 (March 1, 2019). https://doi.org/10.7454/jki.v8i1.10399.

Labouret, Henri. "France's Colonial Policy in Africa." *African Affairs* XXXIX, no. CLIV (January 1940): 22–35. https://doi.org/10.1093/oxfordjournals.afraf.a100972.

Macgovern, Mike. *Making War in Côte D'Ivoire*. Chicago: University Of Chicago Press, 2011.

Mayer, Nonna. "From Jean-Marie to Marine Le Pen: Electoral Change on the Far Right." *Parliamentary Affairs* 66, no. 1 (2013): 160–78. https://doi.org/10.1093/pa/gss071.

McGowan, Patrick J. "African Military Coups d'État, 1956–2001: Frequency, Trends and Distribution." *The Journal of Modern African Studies* 41 (August 2003): 339–70. https://doi.org/10.1017/s0022278x0300435x.

Médard, Jean-François. "'La Politique Est Au Bout Du Réseau'. Questions Sur La Méthode Foccart." *Les Cahiers Du Centre de Recherches Historiques*, no. 30 (October 30, 2002). https://doi.org/10.4000/ccrh.612.

Medushevskiy, Nikolay A, and Alisa R Shishkina. "Modern French Policy on the African Continent: Transformations of a Françafrique Model." *Journal of Asian and African Studies* 57, no. 6 (September 19, 2021): 002190962110462. https://doi.org/10.1177/00219096211046275.

Melly, Paul. "Why France Faces so Much Anger in West Africa." *BBC News*, December 5, 2021, sec. Africa. https://www.bbc.co.uk/news/world-africa-59517501.

Meredith, Martin. *The Fate of Africa : From the Hopes of Freedom to the Heart of Despair : A History of Fifty Years of Independence*. Public Affairs, 2005.

Moncrieff, Richard. "French Africa Policy: Sarkozy's Legacy, and Prospects for a Hollande Presidency." *South African Journal of International Affairs* 19, no. 3 (December 2012): 359–80. https://doi.org/10.1080/10220461.2012.741104.

Mortimer, Gavin. "Macron Can't Escape Blame for France's Failures in Africa." The Spectator, August 9, 2023. https://tinyurl.com/ypxjhux7.

Noubel, Filip. "'Françafrique': A Term for a Contested Reality in Franco-African Relations." Global Voices, February 5, 2020. https://tinyurl.com/2s4xennb.

Oğurlu, Ebru. "EUROPEAN NEO-COLONIALISM in AFRICA." *Uluslararası Politik Araştırmalar Dergisi* 4, no. 2 (August 30, 2018): 1–21. https://doi.org/10.25272/j.2149-8539.2018.4.2.01.

Pascal Airault, and Jean-Pierre Bat. *Françafrique*. Tallandier, 2019.

Perottino, Michel, and Petra Guasti. "Technocratic Populism à La Française? The Roots and Mechanisms of Emmanuel Macron's Success." *Politics and Governance* 8, no. 4 (December 17, 2020): 545–55. https://doi.org/10.17645/pag.v8i4.3412.

Perspective Monde. "Discours Du Président Français François Mitterrand Sur La Démocratisation En Afrique | Evenements | Perspective Monde," June 20, 1990. https://tinyurl.com/3p5buhhn.

Pitcher, Anne, Mary H. Moran, and Michael Johnston. "Rethinking Patrimonialism and Neopatrimonialism in Africa." *African Studies Review* 52, no. 1 (April 2009): 125–56. https://doi.org/10.1353/arw.0.0163.

Powell, Jonathan M, and Clayton L Thyne. "Global Instances of Coups from 1950 to 2010: A New Dataset." *Journal of Peace Research* 48 (March 2011): 249–59. https://doi.org/10.1177/0022343310397436.

Powell, Jonathan, Abigail Reynolds, and Mwita Chacha. "A New Coup Era for Africa?" ACCORD, March 2022. https://tinyurl.com/y2eu524a.

Rodney, Walter. *How Europe Underdeveloped Africa*. Verso, 2018.

Seibt, Sébastian . "Friends at Any Price: China Seeks Allies, Arms Markets in West Africa as French Influence Wanes." France 24, August 26, 2023. https://tinyurl.com/p76d7zxk.

Shin, Won Yong. "[PDF] French Foreign Policy towards Africa under Jacques Chirac by Shin, Won Yong · 2287276104 · OA.mg." *Oa.mg* 3, no. 2 (December 1, 2010): pp 75-89. https://oa.mg/work/2287276104.

Siradağ, Abdurrahim. "Understanding French Foreign and Security Policy towards Africa: Pragmatism or Altruism." *Afro Eurasian Studies* 3, no. 1 (June 1, 2014): 100–122. https://tinyurl.com/497y49ka.

Souaré, Issaka K. "The African Union as a Norm Entrepreneur

on Military Coups d'État in Africa (1952-2012): An Empirical Assessment." *The Journal of Modern African Studies* 52 (2014): 69–94. https://www.jstor.org/stable/43302097.

Staden, Cobus van. "China's Growing Influence in West Africa." The China Global South Project, November 10, 2022. https://tinyurl.com/4n9eapn6.

Startin, Nicholas. "Marine Le Pen, the Rassemblement National and Breaking the 'Glass Ceiling'? The 2022 French Presidential and Parliamentary Elections." *Modern & Contemporary France* 30, no. 4 (November 11, 2022): 1–17. https://doi.org/10.1080/09639489.2022.2138841.

Tastan , Necva . "Türkiye, Russia, China Could Fill Void Left by France in Africa: Professor." Anadolu Agency , September 14, 2023. https://tinyurl.com/2xfzrcjv.

The Economist. "What Have French Forces Achieved in the Sahel?," February 14, 2022. https://tinyurl.com/4uenfkpx.

Thomas-Johnson, Amandla. "Why Is Anti-French Sentiment Spiking in Senegal Protests?" www.aljazeera.com, March 12, 2021. https://tinyurl.com/msecxrwx.

Touati, Sylvain . "FRENCH FOREIGN POLICY in AFRICA: BETWEEN PRÉ CARRÉ and MULTILATERALISM ." *Chatham House. An Africa Programme Briefing Note*, February 2007. https://tinyurl.com/2czwzkny.

Turpin, Frédéric. "Jacques Foccart et Le RPF En Afrique Noire, Sous La Ive République." *Les Cahiers Du Centre de Recherches Historiques*, no. 30 (October 30, 2002). https://doi.org/10.4000/ccrh.572.

Utley, Rachel. "France and the Chad Crisis: superpower-proxy interventionism in Africa." Review of International Studies 17.2 (1991): 131-148.

Vermersch, Lucie Viviane Danielle. "Framing Immigration and National Sovereignty in the French Far-Right: Marine Le Pen's Rhetoric and the Dédiabolisation Strategy." Knowledge UChicago, June 2022. https://knowledge.uchicago.edu/record/3732.

Verschave, François-Xavier. La Françafrique: Le plus long scandale de la République. Stock, 1998.

Vision of Humanity. "Terrorism in the Sahel | Global Terrorism Index 2022." The Global Terrorism Index 2022 produced by Institute for Economics & Peace., April 21, 2022. https://tinyurl.com/y6un4km3.

Williamson, Lucy . "France Islam: Muslims under Pressure to Sign French Values Charter." *BBC News*, December 1, 2020, sec. Europe. https://www.bbc.co.uk/news/world-europe-55132098.

About the Author

Hichem Karoui is a social scientist researcher, political analyst, consultant, novelist, poet, English-Arabic Editor-in-Chief and author or co-author of over fifty published books and numerous academic or media articles. He holds a PhD in Sociology from The Sorbonne University (Paris III).

Research Interests:
- Macrosociology: Elites, Conflicts, Power Building, Islam, China, USA, Russia, Arab World, Social theory, AI, and the Post-Modern World.
- Microsociology: Sociology in Day-to-Day Life (self-improvement, happiness, business, time management, technology, health, etc...).

Experience:
-Founder and Director of GEW Reports and Analyses (The Voice of the Mediterranean), France-based think tank and Online publishing platform.
- Researcher and Consultant for "Underscore Media" in Abu Dhabi (2019-February 2023).
- Director of the Gulf Future Center in London (January 2020 - October 2022).

- Non-resident Senior Fellow and academic adviser at various institutions in China (2019-2021).

- Researcher and Consultant at the Diplomatic Institute, Doha (2013-2019).

- Associate Researcher at the Arab Center for Research and Policy Studies, Doha (2011-2013).

- Researcher at the Sorbonne University's Centre for Contemporary Oriental Studies, Paris (2009-2011).

- Journalist, commentator, Editor-in-Chief, political analyst, and columnist (1981-2019).

Scholarly Publications:

- Author of multiple books on various topics, including On China And the Arabs, The Political Algebra of Global Value Change, Power Revolving Doors , Self-Improvement, What is Happiness, Middle East Studies in the USA, Inventing The Middle East, etc.

- Published numerous articles and research papers in peer-reviewed journals and international conferences.

He has also written several literary works, such as the serialised novel "The Morning of the Mogul."

In addition to his academic and literary pursuits, Karoui has worked as a journalist, commentator, editor-in-chief, political analyst, and daily or weekly columnist in Arabic and English for various media outlets in the Arab world, Europe, the United States, and China.

Academic Degrees:
- PhD in Sociology, Sorbonne University (Paris 3).

- MA in Middle Eastern and Mediterranean Studies, Sorbonne University (Paris 3).

- Maitrise (Master 1) in English Language, Literature, and Civilisation, Sorbonne University (Paris 3).

- Maitrise (Master 1) in Arabic Language, Literature, and Civilisation, Sorbonne University (Paris 3).

www.ingramcontent.com/pod-product-compliance
Lightning Source LLC
Chambersburg PA
CBHW071240020426
42333CB00015B/1565